"A most welcome ludibrium, *Co*[...]
of close-riveted situationist, alche[...]
into an imagined unconscious i[...]
Flesh-and-blood Alien Leonard Rossiter's animation of
two sitcom masterpieces, plus the early-to-mid-70s BBC
Ghost Stories for Christmas and unforgettable *Stone Tape*
play, are all revealed as indicative low/high-lights of the
memorable void that was 1974. Sophie Sleigh-Johnson's
book is a lament for lost times and perceptions, extruded
through the clinging metaphor and symbolism of damp...
Code: Damp is both a handsome response to national
decline and a celebration of hidden arts emerging from
a long scream in the bog. Soaked in disappointment, the
Decadent imagination with all its wondrous esotericism
breathes through this fast-paced book like Paul Simon's
prophecy on tenement halls, Philip K Dick's observation
that 'the symbols of the divine show up in our world
initially at the trash stratum', or Blake's vision that 'God
is in the lowest effects as well as the highest causes'. Sophie
Sleigh-Johnson tugs us into the comic murk in quest of
liberating spiritual light: sole, if ambiguous solace from
'the post-industrial truth of Britain'. Like Magwitch rising
from the marshes, *Damp* is the Fertile Crescent — and
Ishtar-Sophie's crown."

Tobias Churton, author of *Aleister Crowley*

"A quite unparalleled work by a quite remarkable person.
The fabric under the surface; the fragments under the
whole."

Irving Finkel, author of *First Ghosts*

"Brought here to the surface, to rise and fall again, is a submerged and subverted world of British sitcom, forced to disclose, on its mucky collar, the psychic (in all its senses) residues and stains of military trauma, colonial guilt, musty Rachmanism, fetid marsh air, and an excess of more. Sleigh-Johnson cascades, merry-perilously backwards, through a damp-sodden, graffiti-blemished wall into — what next? — the oldest writing system that disrupts time's arrow and shoots it into its foot. The layers here, levels, strata, decades of wallpaper, rug over carpet, dust under beds and bedrock are Quality Street–worlds ripe for analysis, mud-larking about, and historically and politically tele-visionary, too, as regards the 'permissive society', its champions and detractors and the buildings they rented, bought, squatted or condemned. It's all so unexpected. Situ-dada myth-history delirium at its very very best!"

Esther Leslie, author of *Hollywood Flatlands: Animation, Critical Theory and the Avant-Garde*

"Variously brilliant and thoroughly bonkers, *Code: Damp* is definitely on to something: the dank, mildewy, cobwebby, miasmic atmosphere permeating our classic sitcoms, which in retrospect seem more alarming than funny, seedy rather than hilarious. The book also celebrates the underrated and largely forgotten genius of Leonard Rossiter, whose manic delivery and frantic comic style symbolises everything that is unsettling, everything we'd wish to flinch from, in the field of light entertainment."

Roger Lewis, author of *The Life and Death of Peter Sellers*

"Comedy as Method. Tele-vision as time-travel. Such might be the bylines for this compelling, original — and esoteric — codex. With *Code: Damp*, Sleigh-Johnson has brought all the considerable resources of her expanded artistic practice into productive encounter with the figures and landscapes of 1970s sitcoms. The result? A singular work of occulture that is also an affirmation of the power of the parochial. This is how media studies was always meant to look!"

Simon O'Sullivan, author of *From Magic and Myth-Work to Care and Repair*

"Seeing and hearing the light in the dark damp humour of the British sitcom, bringing the future into past. Which version of yourself do you find in Sophie Sleigh-Johnson's extensive book *Code: Damp*? What she call the holes of social rot, always evident in British society, have lost their supernatural lustre, that would otherwise bring excitement and acceptance of the misery through the paranormal explanations of bad situations and the dark humour that brings relief, the hyper intelligence of the everyday antihero Rigsby juxtaposing the universal university smarts of his lodgers: a precog of things to come in the '90s, when students were the norm and folk stories were buried under new books and shows of shiny surface-level humour. Only the cats feel the damp now, smelling the past pseudo-glory on our shoes. Pestering us to RE-remember the most inane, intrinsic clotted creaminess of British self-deprecating cleverness, she succeeds in celebrating several achievements of storytelling and writing that must never be forgotten."

Eleni Poulou, musician and poet

"LUCIFER ON THE BUSES! *Code: Damp* is one of the strangest books I have read. As well as one of the most evocative, lateral, sidereal... an unspellable jewel. Sophie Sleigh-Johnson has channelled Sir Thomas Browne through a BetaMax video recorder. Showing TONIGHT: Britain's Secret History of Everythings in Nothings, illuminated by the Minor Arcana of Britain's stars of TV screens and dreams, groovy prophets singing in the tat and debris of the Swinging '70s, Queens and Kings in Cardboard. It's Borley Rectory dreamt in Cuneiform, Sad Suburban Satan Sex (the rising damp graveyard of wet dreams). It's Pseudodoxia Epidemica on *Top of the Pops*, and *Carry On*, Grimoires. Even when you think you have read this book, you haven't — and then you'll notice you've already started it again."

David Tibet, founder of Current 93

"A surveyor of historic buildings recently exposed the idea of 'rising damp' as a fraudulent fiction, invented in the early '60s by wide-boy companies whose chemical fixes were useless at best. This splendidly weird book now emerges from the Essex marshes to insist, with the help of flickering TV memories and a wealth of other unexpected sources, that the 'myth' of rising damp was real enough to enter and perhaps take over the English soul."

Patrick Wright, author of *The Sea View Has Me Again: Uwe Johnson in Sheerness*

CODE: DAMP

CODE: DAMP

An Esoteric Guide to British Sitcoms

Sophie Sleigh-Johnson

Published by Repeater Books

An imprint of Watkins Media Ltd

Unit 11 Shepperton House

89-93 Shepperton Road

London

N1 3DF

United Kingdom

www.repeaterbooks.com

A Repeater Books paperback original 2024

1

Distributed in the United States by Random House, Inc., New York.

Copyright © Sophie Sleigh-Johnson 2024

Sophie Sleigh-Johnson asserts the moral right to be identified as the author of this work.

ISBN: 9781915672070

Ebook ISBN: 9781915672438

Printed and bound by CPI Group (UK) Ltd, Croydon, CR0 4YY

Contents

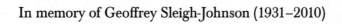
In memory of Geoffrey Sleigh-Johnson (1931–2010)

"No doubt, the damp was rising, and the odour of the earth filled the house, and made such as entered draw back, foreseeing the hour of death."

Arthur Machen

The Prologue

Frankie Howerd's *Prologue* is a Lucretian ripple of ancient affect in the stream of modern television. Slave to the womanising senator Ludicrus Sextus, Howerd's character Lurcio in the BBC sitcom *Up Pompeii!* is the interlocuter from the ancient world to this 1970s spoof, scripted by film franchise *Carry On*'s Talbot Rothwell. Bringing the audience up to date with the comings and goings of the ancient world, Howerd heads up (and, in fact, ends) each episode — I'll leave off from calling it a historical re-enactment — with *The Prologue* addressed to screen, which in turn is always interrupted by Senna the Soothsayer, revealing that week's plot in the form of a prediction. Directly speaking to sitting rooms across mid-century Britain throughout each programme, the repeatedly interrupted prologue's place at the start of each episode makes it a recursive model: a magical frame anticipated by the viewing public, that reinstated Howerd's exceptional fusing of familiar chat show host and ancient world Chorus, of arcane prophesy and inuendo. Two sides of the same coin.

British comic Howerd was by then a familiar face in theatre, radio, TV and the sex comedy films of the time, such as his appearances in the British toilet surrealism of the *Carry On* franchise. He had been in stage musical *A Funny Thing Happened on the Way to the Forum* in 1963 (a gauche Roman romp with hints of Roman playwright Platus) just before Michael Mills and Tom Sloan from BBC Comedy and Light Entertainment visited the ruins of Pompeii. One remarked to the other that he half expected Howerd to come round the corner of a wall. Why not?

His appearance in the resulting *Up Pompeii!* (exclamation mark is crucial) gave Howerd a fund of matey acceptance upon which to draw, creating a "situation" in the glaring heat of the TV studio. As Richard Dyer's 1973 *Light Entertainment* BFI Television Monograph said, television audiences preferred this "television situation" that brought the host into the metaphoric zone of the watcher, underlined by the "relayed interaction situation" of the studio audience's reaction. A trope of much mid-century light entertainment television shows, Howerd's coalescence of darts master caller, live club manager and pre-recorded broadcaster is the mica in late entertainment's disintegrating ground rock.

Howerd always seemed like he was playing a weird cameo anyway, highlighting the uniqueness of his role in *Pompeii!* A masochistic outsider, Howerd's infamous life-long delivery style of *oohs* and *aahs*, not to mention constant conspiratorial fourth-wall-breaking asides and insults to the audience, were allegedly the result of an error in his early script reading, that became habit. Brought in to provide punctuation pauses by writer Erik Sykes, Howerd included them in the delivery to create a syncopated glossing of word and gesture, of force and form. His comic style reaches its gauche zenith in *Up Pompeii!*, breaking down the barrier of TV audience and performer, with an almost Theatre of Cruelty bombast that French surrealist and Modern dramatist Antonin Artaud would have been proud of.

Well played.

Howerd, speaking in 1990, again addresses himself to an imaginary viewer in *Arena*'s "Oooh Er, Missus!" The citizens of Southend in Essex had *him* to thank for their life and livelihoods:

> *"I was in the army, in the earlier days of the war; we did shows in Shoeburyness in the Garrison Theatre there, and it went very well.*
>
> *"And so — the entire defence of Southend-on-Sea and it's 200,000 inhabitants was entrusted to me, Frankie Howerd!*
>
> *"I must've been a formidable soldier, because Southend was never invaded, and I know how grateful they were."*

Shoeburyness abuts Southend's eastern Essex marshes: a mephitic place, lurking on the far reaches of both Borough and consciousness. Here, the divinations of Senna the Soothsayer are replaced with the prophetic forces not just of local nineteenth-century Cunning Men,[1] but of the Essex landscape as a significant agency.

Marsh improved.

Code: Damp will be at pains to suggest that oracular geomantic pattern predates Howerd's vaudeville, because it's found in the magical operativity of Essex mud itself: the metaphysics

---

1 Infamous Thames Estuarine Hadleigh-based Cunning Murrell (1785–1860) was one such figure: a seemingly anachronistic but, in reality, no doubt congruent throwback to days of counter-sorcery and herbalism; his reputation is now suffocated under yards of local history self-publishing and psychogeographic sand bagging.

of material writ large as if the landscape were projected on a screen, as an older technology. Although bawdily benign at the time, the now evidently mercurial atmosphere of *Up Pompeii!* stems from a similar combination — an ancient location and the technology of the television — to invocate that landscape's past.

Comedy as mode most exemplifies this affect, with Frankie Howerd recounting that during his RADA interview, he was dismissed as "*not 1966*" (not vogueish or commodifiable), and that he had "the musty ambience of a bygone age, the mouldy patina of incipient decay". Something in his off-stage banter, his weird punctuation, his embodiment, haunts the interviewers, but more importantly, the screen. Fittingly, as the baseline of this entire book, this patina of damp's legend is where a stamp of comic disjointedness transforms into esoteric meaning. This book takes very seriously the idea that the sitcom is this supernatural structure of ancient things made into electric vision: "I felt like something Mortimer Wheeler [British archaeologist] had dug up," Howerd concludes. Wheeler, a British archaeologist, was fittingly, "the embodiment of popular archaeology through the medium of television".

This book extends this reading of technological artefacts (within, not a single sentence wasted on Victorian ghosts and Spiritualism) via landscapes ancient and modern, using the British sitcom as model for experiencing esoteric yet quotidian rhythms, which in so doing, prioritise the weirdness of popular culture. Certain artefacts project through centuries and across the spiritual billboards of Modernity. This is the route I've taken out of my insuperable but striven failure to interfuse impressions, inscriptions, marsh tidal pulls, increases in beer percentage, jokes, even carrier bag crackle, and transcribe it into the writing on the wall, to communicate the eerie empiricism of sense phenomena, the heaviness of light entertainment.

Part 1's exposition of the sitcom *Rising Damp* takes writing in the most expanded of senses — and its evidence in the eponymous damp — as a form of domestic yet esoteric writing, a textual production that finds its way into mystical practices across centuries, underlined by the marsh as both real and imagined landscape. In Part 2, the sitcom *The Fall and Rise of Reginald Perrin* mobilises this production through a potential of the parochial as site and method of modern myth. Perrin weaponises the parochial through tactics of the hermetic every day, which is also illustrated through archaeologised topographies of pub, commute, office and their attendant accessories: trowels, photocopiers, dart boards.

Being a local reporter for a small free Essex newspaper since my late twenties expurgated geologic and social patterns and stoked an art school *détournement* of this specifically local surrealism. Chance humour and weirdness to ease the burden of employment, between taking collage impressions of Tory councillors on my out-of-date cassette Dictaphone, to photocopying my cuneiform tablet on their photocopier, to hours post-work watching *Minder* slightly inebriated. Many locations in the book have also been visited by me as "psychic researcher reconnaissance": a set of damp pilgrimages where fragments of text, Dictaphone recordings and collected ephemera add a palimpsest of experience to landscapes of earth and text — outputs that result in tape collage and visual work as much as writing. A parochial methodology — borne of an allergy to specialisation — that also takes research to mean a linguistic and elemental interfusion with places both real and imagined, fuelled by myth's associative magic.

Working from damp on bungalow windowsills and the twilight hours of the vast Thames Estuary backed by the crumbling crack dens and seafront illuminations, set to music with Easter Cantatas, composed this century on an organ out near the Essex marshes.

I've said too much.

As Howerd embodied an anachronistic presence within the noise of broadcast, so the mercurial acting of British comic actor (and Howerd's contemporary) Leonard Rossiter is *Code: Damp*'s focus. His outline is a Mr Punch-like shadow from watching television at my church organist grandfather's home. TV phenomena are spectral, in as much as they embody and throw out in the present's air an ancient feeling, a potential of an alterne dimension to existence, which briefly assumes the costume of the domestic consumer electronic. How to do justice to the maniacal potential encoded in the stains of a living room carpet, that look like a surreal landscape bathed in the TVs glow,[2] or the half-recalled static of the sitcom mingling with familial communion and incipient unease. One answer is to inhabit the blips and gaps of the TV as a modern imperative of time's experience. If noise is the grisaille pattern of static flickering behind the glass screen when no signal is received, this book will try to tune in to a layered stratum of this noise in other forms of material culture, reading its interference as a generative message of other realties: the haunted technics from which the fragile band of code comprising our sense of time, and self, is briefly emitted.

Whilst Leonard Rossiter's two sitcoms are the device, he himself is the "guide" or psychopomp for this route out of the twenty-first century. The ambiguity of my feelings towards

---

2   Hired from Radio Rentals.

the look-back bores, as much to the futility of attempting to capture fleeting projection of reality, is an antagonism that can be useful. Mark E. Smith, vocalist and leader of popular "post-punk" music group The Fall, operative in Manchester from 1976 to his death in 2018, is an important character, showing how to disavow and embody the sitcom's patterns. Rossiter and Smith, not forgetting the spectral shimmer of Rigsby (Leonard Rossiter's most famous comic creation in *Rising Damp*) occasionally coalesce in my mind as one. Perhaps mirror shard reflections of a greater spirit that is the weird parlour game of Modernist consciousness. But it's not even that weird — it's a professional stoicism tinged with the mercurial Code, which glimmers on the edges of reality like an out-of-focus photograph, rather than forcing itself imposingly, and with unimpeachable verisimilitude, on the consciousness.

Mark E. Smith's lyrical and atmospheric collage *sacrae*, the fusing and disarranging of timelines and glimmers plucked from a hermetic Prestwich whirlpools into previously unknown "ficta" and incidentals, exemplify this pattern.[3] Not only he, but other players flicker through the script: Paranormal investigator T.C. Lethbridge, Protestant Reformation boss Martin Luther, Victorian Welsh occult writer Arthur Machen, British actor and TV archaeology presenter Tony Robinson, comic actor Rik Mayall, Essex-based occult researcher and writer Andrew Collins, Heteroclite religious novelist Fr. Rolfe, Fifth Monarchist Anna Trapnell, the Chuckle Brothers, Alan Partridge... as well as theorists including Mark Fisher, Bernard

---

3　My grandfather Geoffrey, as above, is also one of these splinted reflections: a benign spirit, a landlord to lodgers in his small Essex home, a friend of the Holston Pils can, an Essex Gnostic meting days out in beatific composition.

Stiegler and Georges Bataille: major and minor arcana in *Code: Damp*'s esemplastic Mystery Play across the centuries. All given parity regardless of their real or fictional status, as art and life bleed here. The imagined is not necessarily reality's correlate and negative, anyhow; Modernity has a habit of both affirming these distinctions but predetermining their enmeshment. Corralling the textures of everyday life, channelling *not too little just enough* (as C.J. in the sitcom *Reginald Perrin*, says) of another dimension, these spirit guides have elevated the grit of the pavement and the communion of the pub into a flickering glimpse of reality's hallucinatory richness.

If a consequence of the hyper-connected world has been at once the proliferation and elevation of previously spurned "genres" like science fiction, fantasy, horror and the supernatural (although some mid-twentieth-century genres like Robert Aickman's self-named "weird stories" are an appropriately serpentine bent, in relation to this globalised trend), the sitcom has yet, I think, to "benefit" from the inevitable reappraisal concomitant with a culture starved of a more original imagination.

Code: Damp's two halves mirror the structure of the (I)TV sitcom as a broadcast, with a dividing commercial break in the form of Leonard Rossiter's own hagiography. Hagiographic texts chart, in medieval hyperbole, the life of a Saint, charting preternaturally superhuman rhythms to actions, signs and untimely deaths (Rossiter died in the dressing room of London's Lyric Theatre in 1984). As quasi-spiritual guide, Rossiter is the magician who galvanises the power of damp's inscription across life and art and allows the time-travel methodologies hinted at when turning these pages, its texture increasingly accelerated, compressed, absurd: Akkadian fortune-telling and English mysticism, pub-soaked sports editing, laugh-a-minute golden comedy moments and advert spiritualism enter you into a slipstream to lost worlds. Read this then as an adept would his arcane text, and Lo, we will discover the true occult landscapes underlying Britain's TV history.

Southend-on-Sea, The Ides of March, MMXXIV

PART 1
Rising Damp

Noise 1

Off-licences are an unwritten rule... as I trip into the Big News 2 past newspaper stands, pages brittle and yellow, martyrs to pies and relics of the bum, the ooze of routine is countered by a muddy presence... alchemy of shops meets the threshold of death.... The abstracted worlds of yours, locally.

Flattening Time

1974

Britcoms? No thanks. I lost faith after *The Chuckle Brothers*.

But *Rising Damp*, produced by Yorkshire Television between September 1974 and May 1978, is a different box of frogs. The scene: a "mucus landlord" benignly terrorises his tenants in the vacuum-sealed world of a preternaturally dingy four-storey. No one goes anywhere much. From the window is the view of the abattoir, the slag heaps and the gasometer: the unacceptable face of bedsitter landlordism, indexed in three symbols of industrial Britain. The two student lodgers — naïve medical student Alan (played by Richard Beckinsale, in a role that is almost the mirror to his part in the concurrent series *Porridge*) and urbane Philip (Don Warrington), who tricks Rigsby into thinking he's an African chief — make occasional reference to their studies but largely conduct their affairs around the centrifugal shared loft bedroom. The downstairs spinster Miss Jones (Frances de la Tour) frets over doilies and keep-fit routines. The holes of social rot are held together by peeling lintels and green walls, presided over by Rigsby, who bursts into his tenants' rooms whilst managing simultaneously to stagger backwards. With Hallowe'en slack jaw and popping eyes, his prurient mithering helps him bemoan the loss of cultural standards, as he sees them, in 1974.[1]

---

1   Today's landlord, on the other hand, is a faceless housing company who has paid off the council, an incipient reality in David Peace's historical

Metonymy both of Rigsby's misery and the fragile state of existence, the *Rising Damp* sitcom set, designed by Colin Pigott, is a stand-in for all old, decrepit buildings that absorb groundwater in the lower sections of walls. With these structural complaints, water rises through capillaries in masonry, saturating the wall surface, up towards the roof. An imprint in tell-tale clouds and sprays of living mould bleeding through its ascent to the surface, incrementally forming and dissolving, undermining stability and surety in a psychedelic mush of hardcore.

Damp is an affective state of this torrid living, a provisional shoring up against the inevitable. As a trace of time's gradual accretion, Rigsby's damp is like a crop mark, a remainder gradually revealing ancient patterns waiting beneath the surface. Within the confines of this TV sitcom, it is a broadcast whose affective sense and message go beyond the merriment of the fast-paced script. Something more sinister seems to keep cutting out the message, like the slurring incursion of digital interference on an old digitised VHS tape of late 2000s pop archaeology programme *Time Team*. Comic presenter Tony Robinson's voice gets distorted, recursively instantiating the difficult process of relaying the past:

TONY ROBINSON: *"How do you know when you've foouuuuund something?"*

... And if you can't, is this the apotheosis of failure? Such occult despair runs through *Rising Damp* as it would through a stick of rock. As do the methods and droves of archaeology

---

fiction trilogy called, appropriately, *Nineteen Seventy-Four*.

itself: a sometimes ludicrous but useful methodology for digging through material layers of the past.

Fast-forward a few decades: after their ebullient success in *The Young Ones* (1982) — a violently surreal cabaret of student digs featuring five college undergrads — lead comic actors Rik Mayall and Adrian Edmondson's follow up 1990s BBC sitcom *Bottom*, plumbed a recognisably joyfully similar (albeit post-Thatcher) crumminess. As Edmondson commented, it wasn't just the scatological opportunity of the sitcom title, but the profound depths of despair implied therein: "We are at the *bottom* of hope," he explained, of their largely autobiographical characters Richie and Eddie. In each episode, they circumnavigate the same few paths through a grimy flat, trapsing through metaphorical excrement, which finds Rigsby (Richie, Reggie... the three Rs of Repetition) in the same predicament.

Rigsby, waiting back in 1974, may admittedly live in a house, but it is a "Flat Time", indicative of the psychological entrapment of a form of habitation, the lived temporality of crap flat tenements, but also their attendant valedictory joys.

In the *Bottom* episode "Finger", Richie and Eddie sod off to a hotel on a stolen ticket, and pretend to be newlyweds. A carry on in the stiflingly old-fashioned hotel restaurant features Richie doing impressions, including one of Rigsby from *Rising Damp* — an awful rendition of the latter's imploring "Oh, Miss Jones...". The French waiter tells Richie and Eddie, "We do a very good red mullet," to which the latter replies: "Oh really? He does a very good Leonard Rossiter." Rigsby's durational performance of dissatisfaction indexed in this oft-repeated impression (repeated in numerous sitcoms) is in part in reference to his longing for said Jones, his upstairs tenant. To live a life at once torrid and luxurious, to sit with the discomfort, would admit the necessary, yet duplicitous, hair shirt: a feature metaphorically donned at all times by Rigsby in his hol(e)y sleeveless cardigan, prowling his boarding house, prophesising the terminus of a social fabric he fails to recognise never existed: a minimal difference between two things as a key hallmark of comedy.

> RIGSBY: *It's an old house this, many dark strange things can happen. There's been a lot of unhappiness here, you now.*
> ALAN: *I've got news for you Rigsby; there still is!*

Bottom's 1990s nesting of sitcom reference, a fictional and factual acknowledgement of the transmission, like a trans-generational ague, of the comic but meaningful history of losers, is a celebration of their relentless endeavours. The "Circular Time" of the working class is the daily grind, which has to wait for the festival to come around. You can't always get what you want, and those that eschew mechanistic sanity and comfort slave at a more alchemical furnace. For such reasons, Rigsby is an artist, an exponent of the "ludic revolution": "What use are creature comforts when the imagination burns?" asks Gordon Comstock's in Orwell's *Keep the Aspidistra Flying* (1936). Rigsby hints at the Janus-faced nuance of the artist's withering existentialism, at once proud of garret-style hard work but reliant on unspoken luxuries, nursing vinegary remembrances.[2]

Rising Damp's metaphoric green and black smears attest to this psychic stain of misery, a material manifestation

---

2   As Shane McGowan sings in the Pogues' song "Bastard Landlord", "Bricks and mortar, Kingdom of Stone/Where do you go when you're all alone?"

of gradual accretion. Indexical to desire's denial, damp is the existential nadir of aspiration. But herein is a grain of galvanising "Vulgar Ecstasies", as Victorian story writer Arthur Machen terms the aesthetics of popular culture, in the betting shop, pub, barrel organ, seaside postcard. Seaside postcards "have an utter lowness of mental atmosphere", but "whatever is funny is subversive", says Orwell lovingly in *The Art of Donald McGill* (1941). Charted through *Rising Damp* — but also *Bottom* and *Carry On* films — is this adversaria of adversity, a subversive power hidden in dark humour. And so Rigsby waits interminably in his tenement, refusing the morphine of seductive consumerism, and like the damp, such eventualities take time to soak in.

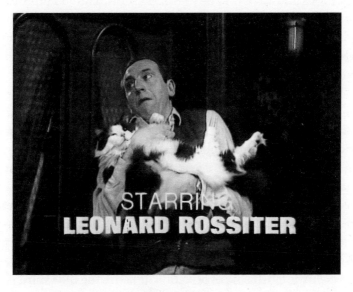

Black Magic.

DARTS MASTER CALLER JOHN McDONALD: That's the sort of failure from which mental blocks start to grow!

Rigsby is also the cardboard cut-out for a feeling of what no doubt seems a male form of disappointment, a declining surety of the ground upon which he stands. Both suspicious of the Eton class who flew the "iron birds" of the Battle of Britain yet ready to ape Churchill's speeches. Scriptwriter Eric Chappell added that the sitcom, which was slated for an American version, never happened: "the bedsit land I portrayed in *Rising Damp* didn't exist in America, so people couldn't relate to it". Rigsby's attitudes form the geological fault line of lower-middle-class Britain of the time, "ingloriously foundering in its own waste products, the backlash and bad karma of empire", as original *Junkie* author William Burrough puts it. In the 1960s and 1970s, "The [Second World] War" manifests a pathology of sentimental esotericism, a not-uncritical Empire nostalgia mirrored in spooky *Dad's Army* colours, a sitcom which in turn was reaching a high point in popularity in the same year, 1974.

Television as a popular broadcast medium developed through the technics of warfare. The BBC's high frequency tube television transmitters were requisitioned back for radars stations, taking entertainment as medium from war and back again. It was during the Second World War that high-fidelity magnetic audio tape was nascently developed, which was to become industry standard for the storing of television images, in a part-abandonment of expensive film stock. Televised entertainment cannot be conceived of without this imbrication in the military-industrial complex. Rigsby's torrid tenement as masochistic fetishising of privation linked to the Blitz spirit is a complicated weaving of mediums. A conditioning of recorded tape. But despite the agon between 1970s sitcom characters, such as *Steptoe and Son* and *On the Buses* painting blokes as sexist and/or losers in contrast to their increasingly enfranchised female counterparts, the nuances of a well-read belligerence and asceticism shouldn't be thrown out with the Anderson shelters, read in the fault lines of Rigsby's penal colony: it is the eponymous *Rising Damp* engrained therein that permits access to a materio-magical form of psychic space at odds with Rigsby's rhetoric of brittle patriotism, attitudes that are demonstrably risible within the sitcom itself. It also cautions against cultural assessors, assuming that his character's little-England xenophobia represents a wholesale viewpoint on the part of the actual actors or scriptwriters.[3]

Rigsby's insensitive and relentless inability to acclimatise to the age and racial difference of his tenants is a constant butt of jokes against him: a focus of the other characters' disdain, something Mark E. Smith of The Fall picked up on. Smith was a "big fan" of *Rising Damp*, as well as of Rigsby and his creator, Leonard Rossiter: the recursive trinity. He said in Austin Collings's *Renegade*: "Pale-minded liberals have moaned subtleties out of *Rising Damp*, as is their wont. Rigsby wasn't all that bad. He's not the bigoted tyke he's been made out to be. He's just a bloke from another generation — a lost sort, looking for company." In reference to the 1980 feature film made from the series — taking the setting to London and a location house in Paddington (and thus, incidentally, losing the magical and dis-placed claustrophobia of the sitcom) — Smith suggests that Rigsby is shown to be "at the centre of a sly sham" when all the other characters are forced to reveal

3   As François Béroalde de Verville says, "beware the hairy paws of the dogmatisers"!

themselves. Up against it on all sides from self-satisfied self-deceivers-all, Rigsby is the only character not playing out a deceit. Smith adds: "I can relate to things like that."

The damp of the house is in it for the long game, as is Rigsby: both attitudes are incommensurate with shallow self-serving posturing; a fact underlined by the self-referential meta-play described by Alan to Rigsby, penned by a thespian lodger in the house:

> RIGSBY: *What's it about?*
> ALAN: *It's a psychological drama — full of symbolism and imagery — played out against a dingy boarding house and dealing with contemporary themes.*
> RIGSBY: *My God — it sounds like another* Play for Today. [4]

The specificity of the nod to another TV production is doubled by its own reference to social-commentary: a generative "pulp modernism" of public broadcasting that tethered visionary terrain to the mildew and furnishing of the everyday. Rigsby, enmeshed in a miasma of middle-aged disappointment, painfully aware of his own crap Englishness, has a narcissism withal tied to an embodied material community that is very material, very damp. The romance of this self-denial is a homing of aberrant strategies, eschewed by glib social climbers labouring under systematised notions of success, that in turn rely on "positivity" as much as clarity. Facile passivity kills this damp and dismal comic spirit, to which there is nothing more inimical than positivity as its Master-Signifier, blunting the edge on which comedy thrives.

---

4   Rossiter starred in two *Play for Today* episodes: "The Factory" (1981) and "Dog Ends" (1984).

RIK MAYALL: What really made me and Ade [Edmondson] laugh was being bad at things.

This is not to say that the deep and multivalent colours of joy and ecstasy are being intellectually or emotionally undermined, but rather that the commercial imperatives of the hyper-industrial drive a pernicious falsity at odds with the reality of the spirit. In *Rising Damp*, failure meets a joy of ludic personal strangeness tinged with the disturbing nature of individuation via the elementality of this creeping damp: as the Abbott says to the Mesopotamian King Nebuchadnezzar in Benjamin Britten's church parable *Burning Fiery Furnace*, "the mettle of man is tried in the furnace of humiliation". Indurate to goth posturing, disconsolate damp reaches further back than any aesthetic movement, and it is a shallow façade of optimism that is inimical to the rich and esoteric temporal scales that it might offer. This especially in countering forms of digitally fostered symbolic misery. Diagnosed by the late philosopher Bernard Stiegler, symbolic misery is partly endemic to that lack of courage to turn away from shallow path of satisfied success in a world where algorithmic conditioning substitutes the importance of grotty experience.

The merchandise of enslavement won't produce works of art, which exist in the multi-durational realm of the spirit, on its way, perhaps, to the bin. The ancient dualistic religions' attempts to separate light and dark, good and evil, material and spiritual, are salutary intimations of aspiration no less attuned to spiritual salvation if we take a heretically inverted Gnostic viewpoint that it is, in fact, this "drab claustrophobia" where this alchemy of the inner life resides.

But this is not just a region of dim surmises. Low materials — mud, but also, spit, hair, excrement — are entries in French surrealist Georges Bataille's dictionary of "base matter". It was Bataille who oriented an avant-garde interest in such gnomic matter, a debasement through materiality, as part of his wider drive to inject an arcane decadence into an increasingly polarised modern politics of the 1930s – by reigniting, at times with forest-dark sacred fires in his secret society, Acéphale, the practices of ancient mystery religions into the suburbs of Paris. Bataille's self-confessed transference of energies onto the "mythical plane" were the metaphysical and political ramifications of this heretical materialism, seeking to invert a Gnostic take on matter, or *hyle*, as debased, and spiritual as transcendent. Bataille's inversion of high and low shared a rejection popular in the 1930s of the Hegelian prioritisation of "spirit" in favour of bleakly galvanising manifest mess. But this isn't to say it is a simply inversion, a mirroring where the order is an echo of anarchy. The somatic exigencies of damp are a spiritual argot, a world of their own. A mess which continues to pose a durational "recurring insult" to aspiration, dependent upon such unreformable grot.[5]

RIGSBY: I was at my best during the Depression.

Rigsby's movements through the tenement, seen through the flat, brittle plane of a television screen and the hyperbolic terrain of an imagined hinterland of chipboard sets, are a "flat time" hostage to domestic misery, and a weird interminable purgatory of social stagnation. But, aided by the materiality

---

5   "Grot" is the name of Reginald Perrin's (played by Leonard Rossiter) anti-commercial venture, a ludic inversion of the utilitarian and commercially driven in favour of the base: a weird inversion of "excess", of which more in Part 2.

of damp, and the affection shown for the buildings and the characters therein, squalid misery as impediment transforms the question of failure into the form of art, and will make of the damp itself a recalcitrant yet transformative mode of time-travel out of the "flat time" of bedsits and small, grimy flats.

Fair Rents for All

> PETER: *And Squatter told me later that, ah, he'd gone… because he'd had to go.*
> DUDLEY: *I think that's…*
> PETER: *That sums up Squatter for me.*
>
> Derek and Clive (Live)

Decrepit domestic structuring was a holding pattern essential to the forefront of wider radicalism and consciousness-raising groups of the English counterculture. A damp tenement's dismal insufficiency was no doubt the state of many squats and condemned buildings of the 1970s, with damp a common feature still of rented properties, as opposed to owned inhabitations.

Squatting, as a necessary channel through this mire, laid down a British social geography borne out of the not-so-long-ago-built high-rise estates, and the increase of both property prices and land developers corroding the capital. I'll give it to the landlord — he's a much older archetype, a centuries-old practice of lodging. On this front, the lodgers *chez* Rigsby are antiquated, and would have been better off getting involved in the nascent housing associations that developed in the late 1970s, and which gave life to movements including the Family Squatters Advisory Service (FSAS) and the All London Squatters movement (ALS). Political agitation in *Rising Damp* raises its head in Series 1, Episode 7, "Stand Up and Be Counted", where a general election sees everyone operate as a cardboard cut-out of themselves. Whilst Rigsby obviously masquerades as a Conservative Party member, and the students' limply talk about Maoism and the Labour Party surrounded by big-breasted pin-ups and Che Guevara posters, blending into the background of Heinz beans cans on shelves (a grimy impressionist scene across which they move in 2D, except for Rossiter, who cuts through stage space like *"whiplash: his body, his very fingertips seem to dance with a kind of gleeful grace"*). The Conservative candidate, Colonel De Vere-Brown — who keeps mispronouncing his name as "Ragsby" — manages to reverse Rigsby's political affiliations when he complains about the state of the house:

BROWN: *Just look at this place — see the damp? You know what this is, don't you? The unacceptable face of capitalism.*
RIGSBY: *(astounded) What?*
BROWN: *(confidentially) How much does he charge for these places?*
RIGSBY: *What do you mean?*
BROWN: *What are the rents?*
RIGSBY: *Well… six.*
BROWN: *Scandalous! You should take him in front of the rent tribunal.*
RIGSBY: *Now wait a minute.*
BROWN: *Don't worry Ragsby, I understand — frightened of the landlord — nasty piece of work I suppose. Well, we intend to do something about this place when we get in. Probably have it pulled down. Build some flats for single tenants. Stop all this exploitation.*
RIGSBY: *You can't demolish this — it's my home.*
BROWN: *Don't worry — you'll be alright, we'll find a place for you.*

RIGSBY: How can you? I'm the landlord, you great puddin'!
BROWN: What!
RIGSBY: You're supposed to be on my side — you should protect the landlords.
BROWN: Not your sort of landlord.

Meanwhile Alan and Philip are creating red-lettered slogans on white placards: *FAIR RENTS FOR ALL.*

Slogans had been made popular the other side of the Channel in the 1950s and 1960s. A period of politics and intellectual ferment typified by the Situationist International, as a background avant-garde group to the wider student protest in Paris of 1968. Whilst by the time of *Rising Damp*, the Situationist had long disbanded, 1974 was the moment their writing came into the British psyche. The year that channelled *Damp* also saw the print publication of Christopher Gray's *Leaving the 20th Century*: the first English-language anthology of the Situationist International's writings. High-tension lines tethering seemingly inverse strategies for escape, or obliteration — if only for the thirty minutes of the scheduled programme.

Situationism's main focus was capitalist-conditioned urban space, and by extension the places in which we live, or which through contingency are placed and shaped. Rigsby's "miserable hovel", with its domesticity and squalid drudgery, provides a noisome antidote to the hypnotism of consumer convenience.

The Situationist strategy of the *dérive*, coined by its leader Guy Debord, was a "drift" through the city to detach oneself from pre-conditioned trappings of existence. Debord's newly constructed "Situations", formed from this debris of consumer life, were a game "composed of gestures contained in a transitory décor". These situations would be moments displaced from the grimy map of commodity relations to heighten the disorienting intensity of *place*: a route through the city directed by ancient and modern patterns, rather than commercial imperatives. Detaching place from its urban(e) carapace allowed a sinister counter-geography to emerge, driven by the psyche, that set the banal street plan adrift from the industrial town planners and marketeers. The tactics of the everyday formed into a magic trick. Is the corroding of consumer space by evidencing the strange lineaments of an intersubjective space better when the background is formed of Heinz cans? A form of English surrealism where the dank air breeds occultation, and resistance finds more wasteland festival under fetid tenements, when the house becomes a psychotropic model for obliteration, through the operations of decadent damp undoing.

If the Situationists are the Chartreuse of radical, then Alan and Philip are the Buckfast. That said, the social make-up of Rigsby's house does stray close on occasion to the constitution of the squatting community so prevalent in the 1970s, caught between worlds and unsure of their identities. A mixture of bourgeois confusion, bohemians, students and working-class agitators. A radicalism that both dug up not just the metaphysical baseline of the Empire's brick foundations, but channelled the literal Digging and Ranting of the British communitarian movements of the seventeenth century.

57 Varieties of wall stain.[6]

BBC community TV "Anarchist Gardeners": "Squatting takes the waiting out of wanting"

Damp's undermining strategies seep into both structural and affective capillaries, with moisture the symbolic miasma of the soul. *Code: Damp*'s sensibility thrives on paradox and perversity. Rigsby both lauds but corrupts his notion of English identity, a flickering reproach at the centre of the furnace, to match the post-industrial truth of Britain: decay, corruption,

---

6   Cf. PiL, "Banging the Door": What do you want? You're irritating, go away, it's not my fault/That you're lonely/Just look around/I think you'll find that everyone has the same problem/This is not a real home/The walls are so thin, the neighbours listen in, keep the noise down/They're complaining/ Humiliated/You were born and bred/Humble, to the spoon-fed/ Why worry now? You're not dead yet/You've got a whole lifetime to correct it/You're wasting/Admiring, hating, this lot are not happy heroes/Just better actors/A-hundred-and-one dilations/And fifty-seven varieties/Outside with the empties: Keep banging the door.

hallucinatory layers, all now replaced with an unsatisfactory and fragile consumer glamour. Rigsby may sharpen his opinions on the whetstone of hypocrisy, but disarticulates a brittle nationalism with the registers of base matter.

Rigsby's outbursts as he roams both the psychic and structural interior of his boarding house, crisscrossing over crinoline notions of British identity and class, cautions a devolution of despair, hysteria and pedestrian monotony through the scales of damp, all the while ominously sounding this dualistic death-rattle of Britain's industrial world.

Noise 2

Interviewer said: What colours are you broadcast in?
Richard: Voodoo. Performed in an empty Essex churchyard. It's lovely and quiet. I don't get anyone coming and disturbing me…

The Writing on the Wall

A folk politics of the ancient insufflates the radicalism and counter-cultural social expression of 1974. The initiation of the Stonehenge Free Festival, although largely a dubious and eventually dreary new-age showland, was a congregation around a symbolically bizarre structure that clung as much to the entrails of the largely disembowelled pre-permissive society, as Rigsby. *Rising Damp* bedevils the dark side of pop culture's unmoored psychic experiment with its quiet, carpeted and crisp-packet disassembly, alongside its more prehistoric miseries fecundating in damp corners.

> *RIGSBY: The permissive society doesn't exist. I should know; I've looked for it.*

The characters in *Rising Damp* only leave the house's walls a handful of times in four series, and twenty-eight episodes. Scriptwriter Eric Chappell made reference to the importance of maintaining the heightened atmosphere of the dingy confines, psychologically and narratively. "It was a very claustrophobic show and I wanted to prove that we could take the show outside the house and it would still work.... But everyone had been so alarmed by filming away from the house that I didn't make a habit of it."

Working its magic, the humdrum smears of the house are an attractor that kept the residents housebound, a different form of mystical experience to the experimentation of the so-called permissive society. Where early modernity had its own specific brand of highly organised occulture in such groups as the Hermetic Order of the Golden Dawn, and its poster boy Aleister Crowley with his practice of magick as self-transformation, by 1974, the *Hammer Horror* meets *Carry On* pulp of 1960s far-out witchery and Wicca dabbling was becoming a deterritorialised heritage commodity. The 1970s were, so I've been told, a browner, post-counterculture mirage. Earlier escapism was more swallowable than the still-lingering filthy carpets of a Dickensian tenement. A relationship between youth and cultural outdatedness symbolised by Rigsby's own fungus-like interior screens.

Rigsby's taciturn loathing for younger forms of Briton was the death-rattle of "something lost" in Arcady. The permissive society promised unbridled leisure time, with the triumph of cultural materialism the coda of the post-industrial lie. Radical strains of Ye Olde England, as a virtual hum or background, nonetheless, pierced the squalor with febrile hymning, as rotten spectre at the feast. The writing was on the wall of a counter-culture that slid happily into mass consumerism, whilst a decade later turning the popular camera inwards to a rural-horror inflected "folk horror" trend in British film and TV was, by focusing on the spookiness of archaeology, enacting a partial dig on itself, making technology an archaeological dig of the twentieth century. The post-dated attribution of the folk horror genre is electrical rigging support for the eerie powers of pre-enlightenment topographies, muddy and psychic. This epochal horror, that at the time was a post-war return to occulted patterns in paganism and modernity, is in contemporary consciousness mired in its own horror scandals, such that the recursive layering of past and landscape through technology takes on a nightmarish diegesis, abetted by the history of the BBC "wiping" TV tape stock for re-use.

Rigsby's overpopulated crumbling house as a structure represented the misery of the past, in contrast to the supposable liberation of modern prefabs and the grey tower blocks of the 1960s, such as the long since flattened Brutalist Oliver Close Estate in Leyton. The view from this huge monolith was depicted in "The Minder" (1972) for the TV Play series *The Frighteners*. This short episode, terse with hypnotic shots, replays the slow-motion dance of a gun cartridge bouncing on railway sleepers and a freight carriage repeatedly rolling into a collision with train stock, as hermetic augur of the high-rise blood about be spilt. A brutal voice breaking the drab reverie of evening sun over the thousands of inhabitants, describes a recent jailbreak: "*He wouldn't want to get socially adjusted, would he? He's dissatisfied, feeling bitter; solitary makes you personally very violent indeed*". Thus spake Brian Glover in his role as gangland boss, a sinister chorus Glover distributes, like character actor Peter Vaughan, across psychological post-industrial horror and comedy — appearing alongside Vaughan in *Porridge* in 1974 (a more benign "doing time"), he also ghosts *Bottom* as the next-door-flat's Mr Rottweiler in 1991. TV plays that can thus loosely be termed "folk horror" stretch the credulity of both the industrial and the bleakly empty as inseperate to the numinosity of ploughed fields.

Peter Vaughan also polarises modernity's affective landscape qualities in Laurence Gordon Clark's directing for the BBC TV series *A Ghost Story for Christmas*. His 1972 adaptation of *A Warning to the Curious*, a ghost story by early Edwardian ghost writer M.R. James, limns the crepuscular weariness of flatland East Anglia. Vaughan's character Paxton — fresh from his role as horrific rural yob in *Straw*

Dogs (1971) — is a down-at-heel amateur archaeologist in pursuit of necromantic meritocracy. Although not part of the rarefied world of James's story, the TV adaptation nods to the Great Depression (also referenced by Rigsby) and Paxton's impecunious hunger for recognition. His shoes are worn to the bone, and the "boots" character, a lugubrious odd job/ball who haunts the silent creek-side lodgings, gloats in a long take over his shabby belongings. The heavy grief of Paxton's failure is felt in the salt-impacted estuary B&B, shots of mantelpieces buzzing with dust and the impervious mudflat wind howling against the windowsills. The little dialogue there is cracks against the landscape: he talks morosely with a hilariously Church of England vicar, the latter dismissive of the weirdly rooted locals; and he desperately pants and gasps whilst unearthing both the ancient Saxon crown of East Anglia and the ghost of its guardian. Curiosity here equates, I think, to the strange mixture of industrial and ancient marsh, a weird de-materialisation that was always evident in these bleak solemn shores, and what has made the shrine of Suffolk a mythological terminus, through the works of M.R. James, but also Benjamin Britten, W.G. Sebald, and latterly, Mark Fisher; a zone from which repeated patterns are drawn, not least in the delineation of disappointed journeymen, as well as a warning to the writer to always keep a collagist method and a sense of humour, lest you get corralled into the more hackneyed solecisms of psychography.

Paxton's shoddy lodgings and their susceptibility to de-materialised occultism are coterminous to the operativity of technology in Nigel Kneale's archetypal BBC TV play *The Stone Tape*, also made in 1972, which indexes the ancient and modern co-presences of the globalised age. An old house's walls are discovered to be the meta/physical baseline of a spectral appearance. In this instance, the stone walls, built on a yet more ancient sacrifice site, posit an arcane form of recording material, discovered by a taskforce of lab-coated scientists from "Ryan Electrics" enlisted in the building to, coincidently, invent a new recording surface. Heightened emotion is the trigger of the screaming spectre: an inorganic memory imbricated both in the stones and in human intentionality. The scientists, chief amongst them head researcher Peter Brock (Michael Bryant, who is also to feature in the 1974 BBC M.R. James adaptation *The Treasure of Abbott Thomas*, aired the same year as *Rising Damp*), gradually realise the room itself is the recorder, with its walls the eponymous tape, as a temporally receptive material: inorganic matter that not only records but re-transmits past events of requisite intensity.[1] They bombard the room with radiophonic bombast to try and alter its coding, but succeed only in "wiping the tape", a recursive reference to the fate of many TV programmes themselves. The hubris — symbolised perhaps in non-diegetic form by the absurdly loud level at which all the actors say their lines — of the commercially driven experimenters is trumped when an ever more arcane record is found resonating in the base matter of the stone. The ancient presence beneath this new recording material requires human sacrifices to sustain the infinite player. A compulsively detached repetition so long as the tape's spooling requires repeated sustenance.

The "Stone Tape Theory" of haunting, so-called, (and wrongly named a "pseudoscience" by scientists and rationalists who think it lays claim to a verifiable state of affairs, rather than a form of active imagination in relation to how the past

---

1   "Are you a behind-the-time modern, or a contemporary of the future?" ask Pauwels and Bergier in *The Morning of the Magicians* (1971).

operates) was popularised following the TV film, but also retroactively attributed to archaeologist, parapsychologist and paranormal investigator T.C. Lethbridge (1901–1971), lauded, not least, by occult thrift shop sifter Colin Wilson. In a number of vaguely parochial and cranky antiquarian works that fused British ghost lore with post-war science, such as *Ghost and Ghoul* and *ESP — Beyond Time and Distance*, Lethbridge laid out "the odd" system. Ghosts were projections stored in materiality, be it rock, stone or water, that both replayed intensely traumatic events in the past, or retroactively played what would happen in the future. It was a case of severe pendulum swinging. Lethbridge was a dab hand at dowsing, and it was primarily magnetic fields of energy, trained at water or mountains, that could act as a medium for recording strong emotions.

The fusty veracity of this practice is the subject of numerous New Age and cod-occult writings and stories: a limited back-alley that misses the wider point to be salvaged from "the odd" system. All the better if Lethbridge had perhaps suggested a swirling pint of beer as the fount of his supernatural *dérive*. Point taken: the reflexive nature of the theory's attribution is early to mid-twentieth-century confusion of technology and aberrant practice in itself. Deep research of this kind never veers far from the hilarious (a key mode of the Code) and Lethbridge came close to *Code: Damp* in his suggestion that "nature" and psyche were collided in node points of place-based intensity. Static electrical zones recursive within landscape drains.

In Essex, circa 1911, at Borley Rectory, reportedly "the most haunted house in Britain", writing from the spirit world by someone called Marianne appeared and was continually re-written over on the walls of a parochial house, emanating from what earlier paranormal investigator and self-made media figure Harry Price speculated to be "psychic ether" — "an intermediate medium between spiritual and physical reality, which can enable objects to carry memory traces of emotions or experiences from the past". Hauntings linked to the particularities of a certain geographical anomaly, like those proposed by T.C. Lethbridge, are like a stain of time, which tethers the small and parochial to vaster terrains: inorganic intent that manifests through the thresholds of *walls* as a transitory medium. It is of note that this TV- and media-inflected ghost sensation occurs in Essex: a key cartography for *Code: Damp*, being, amongst other things, a "damp part of the world", as Georgian writer Daniel Defoe kindly confirms.

Borley Rectory and the house of *Rising Damp* both perform the stain of domestic time. Both in the real bleak English pastoral of the house structure and the heavy weight of the seconds passing, in the sense that something ancient underlines the house. This torrid surrealism has multiple timelines, whose yet darker strains are evident in other artefacts of the period. Although film, and not the terrain of TV, Roman Polanski's 1976 film *The Tenant*, part three of his "apartment trilogy", preceded by *Repulsion* and *Rosemary's Baby*, sees strains of arcane-inflected horror visit the sins of the Enlightenment on

Borley vs ancient cuneiform writing: How do you know when you've found something?

the brown world of the 1970s. Polanski, in the lead role, arrives at the flat, and undergoes a phantasmic transformation into the previous tenant: a moribund female scholar of Egyptology. The hues of the tenement's muddy green and occasional blue and red of his make-up are a Letraset transfer of *Rising Damp*'s decoration. The arcane truth which lurks in the domestic is ratified when Polanski hallucinates Egyptian hieroglyphics appearing on the toilet walls: an outhouse which is the scene of spectral figures who stare at him from within the dunny, over many long nights. The knowledge of how the twentieth century's cultural weight collapses in on us, revealing the past through the spectrum of a technology, far exceeds any time period's right to knowledge thereof.

This is unique in the 1970s: a period of incipient neoliberal melancholy for folk traditions, evidenced in the preponderance of this so-called "folk horror" in TV artefacts above, like *A Warning to the Curious* (1972) but also *Stigma* (1977), *The Children of The Stone* (1977), *Robin Redbreast* (1970), *Penda's Fen* (1974) and *A Photograph* (1977). Whilst some of these are *Ghost Stories for Christmas*, the last three in the list are part of the fourteen-year-long *Play for Today* drama series that the BBC started airing in 1970, and which Rigsby himself lampoons, for being this awkward blurring of TV format and proscenium arch vibe. The *Rising Damp* episode "Stage Struck" concerns a thespian lodger, Hilary, writing a play starring the rest of the tenants, based self-referentially on the damp lodgings.

Folk horror is entranced with landscape as an uncanny stage for the performance of the past, and contestations of land ownership: Pagan and pre-Reformation psychic recording surfaces.

The horror of mid-century high-rises, the empty pastoral of fields quieted by enclosure, overlayed by the 1970s adaptations of marsh shores — M.R. James's occult antimonies generate in bleak landscapes — are all heightened post-war British topographies, as much as ancient symbolisms of the past. The Green Man mysticism of British culture is a metonym of the spirit of place, but is re-written with accelerated mid-century industrialisation as a collective historicism hand in hand with Tudorbethan nostalgia. Magic and place recursively re-write themselves in this tradition, as post-counterculture expurgations of modernity, all the more redolent for their admixture with torrid, industrial locales. Rigsby's lodgings were the embodiment of the historical leap between old Victorian tenancies and cheap utility furniture of the post-war age, but retained traces of misery, the razor-sharp thrill of existence, and the mythic fear industrialised that folk horror as post-dated genre reflects: this is done without a recourse to any rurality as a residue of cyclical rooted paganism. Weird story writer Alan Garner avers, "When Folk and Horror come together, I would say that a chance has been missed. There is enough fear in Folklore naturally for it to serve its purpose, to be constructive and genuine, without the ersatz application of horror."

Georges Bataille's text *The Absence of Myth* (1948) outlines that modernity found cohesion in making a myth of myth's denial. In modernity all mythic and religious systems are contained through the unifying narrative of this absence. In killing God, a new myth has arisen. Mythology determines access to the conditions of the world. The mythology of the 1970s, seen fleetingly in M.R. James adaptations, is importantly demonstrated in *Rising Damp* as traces of mythic fear purposeful through comedy: a specific mode whose marshy substratum is at once archaic *and* modern. Rigsby's walls, nested within the diegesis of the sitcom, *become* a landscape of time's stain themselves. Damp is the text of place, where the comic is this admixture of quotidian and strange, incised in the muddy landscape of British occulture. Laugh tracks laid down in the hyperbolic mud alchemise the base matter of the process, the "Great Work" to demonstrate Frankie Howerd's imbrication of time's patina of "incipient decay" and comedy.

This force of humour organises our bodies, our thoughts, traversing the previously thought distinction between writing and surface, and the intersection of fiction, cultural artefacts and life. Damp rising up and out of the walls, it is a strange hallucinatory force behind the experience of space and time, both before and after popular culture's structuring. This is the bog-standard truth which *The Stone Tape* had already admitted four years before *Rising Damp* aired: a drab and haunted home's walls are the only site for ancient correspondences to manifest a sinister grammatology – a damp marshy landscape as the legend of a heavy and technology-saturated 1970s.

Noise 3

...Proto Stonehenge by Verger "on the want", Live excavation broadcast through the back of England... Relatively good quality, though smearing test card.

De(sur)facements

The crawling of damp on a wall at once daws attention to yet defaces its spatial surface: constructive destruction, confirming that the stain, the growth, has a sense of depth and movement important to the framing of ground and figure. Graffiti as a regime of inscription is both textual production and willed defacement. Like damp, it both destroys and produces, operative as both. Such defacement of a surface, when read as this textual production, was commonly more "acceptable" in the Middle Ages. Church walls were scrapbooks, a palimpsest of music notation, cartoons and drawings for a largely illiterate populace. Insignia combining folk magic, evil eye signs, mnemonics, jokes, auspicious dates. Inscription in this form accords import to the material and geographical location of inscription as much as to semantic meaning. These minor drawn gargoyles are cognate with the more auspicious fabric of the building: a parity that takes the fustiness out of the holy setting.

Fifteenth- and sixteenth-century texts also attest to the prevalence of wall inscription, such as "candle writing" — smoky pillow talk eked out as "Cheape candle bawdry" onto chamber walls, testament to a world structured by light and shadow. This, too, was as prevalent as carving in window frames, doors and passages. Even the alehouse walls were more akin to a disarticulated codex, with ballads and pamphlets pasted across them. With a relaxed attitude to structural fabric, buildings become vast texts, a surrealist imagining of blown up and preternatural script — chased later in the production of pamphlets during the English Civil War as a poster rendering of the Renaissance Memory Palace.

The ribald and heartfelt inscription covering both domestic

and public quarters in the early modern period seems to create a perpetual *vox pop*. What were personal witticisms and ribald thrifty sentences in the seventeenth century, biblical phrases and bon mots, have become giftshop phrases, festooned over hanging placards and mug coasters for the terminally unimaginative to bear witness to writing's power. Keep Calm and Carry On. Carry on What? *Convenience*? The 1971 outing of the popular film franchise was located in a toilet factory, resurfacing popular culture on pink bog roll. This cheap WC bawdrey, from Charles Hawtrey, stops graffiti writing being too Merrie Englande, as luckily, *the writing on the wall* is often as not the writing in the stalls: bogside visions inscribed on public toilet cubicles goes hand in hand with the advent of public and private spaces in the later modern period.

The Situationist International used external urban graffiti to both mark on and draw up latent presences in building fabric and its attendant psyche. Their infamous graffito critiquing capitalism's spatial flattening determinants, "Underneath the pavement, the beach" (*Sous les pavés, la plage*),[2] when scrawled in spray-can ink underneath a Parisian shopping window inculcates *les pavés* — cobblestones — as sacred rocks that are not only ancient script surfaces, but potentially a *mise-en-scène* for drawing up metastable, abyssal potential always at deep play underneath the usual reality. The text is drawn, albeit flush in sprayed ink, to re-surface a powerful force in places, and in so doing, makes the concrete wall a transitory

---

2 "I don't wanna holiday in the sun/I wanna go to new Belsen/I wanna see some history/'Cause now I got a reasonable economy!/Now I got a reason, now I got a reason/ Now I got a reason, and I'm still waiting/ Now I got a reason/Now I got reason to be waiting... the Berlin Wall."

Vision in the Void.

fabric, a time-travelling medium, and the spray can a tool of supernatural archaeology: in effect a retroactive digging of words from the past into the future. Another Situationist graffito — *Ne Travaillez Jamais* ("Never Work!"), described by Christopher Gray as "one of the most important relics ever unearthed on the site of Saint-Germain-de-Prés" — is a figure on the ground of memory, at play — literally — under the pavements, to escape the imposed consumerist hegemony of the city.

Such escape is charted though erstwhile Situationist Asper Jorn's book *Signes gravés sur les églises de l'Eure et du Calvados*. His notion of an "Comparative Vandalism" came full circle, bringing the industrial quotidian back to the ancient parish, tracing a gnomic yobbo impulse in Viking graffiti across Medieval churches in Normandy. Many otherwise eerily dismal Normandy flatlands are peppered with very similar looking churches, uniquely defaced with these carvings. The outer walls are like a stone page, adorned with crosses, faces, hands, fish and hermetic symbols, and the three-headed

Yobbo Impulse, Normandy.

Baphomet icons as worshipped by the Knights Templar. Jorn, having noticed these in Normandy, and the same class of marks in churches across Denmark, Sweden and Norway, on the cathedrals of Ribe, Lund and Trondhjem, read them as routes of migration set in hard stone walls, making the parietal articulation a living poly-dimensional emigration map.[3]

This urge to fill "space" disavows the assumption of the flat surface of the writing support, but partakes in a live erosion of sacred and profane: church walls, as much as boozer interiors and toilet noticeboards, accord an effervescence of approach removed from the heritage sanitation of Perspex protections and other methods of "Egyptianising", viz suppressing, the past. All the above graffiti can be read as a

---

3   Evidence of which I saw on a trip through the departments of Calvados and Eure, using Jorn's heavy text as guidebook.

(criminal) defacement, but in drawing attention to the duality of a support surface and the figure traced thereupon, shows a co-constitutive maddening process of something being re-surfaced as much as imposed upon: a defacement, but a revelation of, in popular culture, a potentially timeless depth to that surface.

If time is materially indexed in stone, mud (and ultimately, damp), its surfacing on supports — like Rigsby's walls — makes the writing a temporal intervention. A site between matter and idea, between, even, an immanent and transcendent function of inscription. The revealing of a layered temporality, the activating of a metaphysical palimpsest within the surface could, with the vandalism of graffiti in mind, be posited as a *de(sur)facement*, in fact, whereby both the surface is remade, but also defaced, at once. Attendant on this is the intent of a mystical effect to the operation, which isn't necessarily implicit in the examples of graffiti on the alehouse, or the church.

Bringing together the inscriptive violence of the defacer, and the magical intent of the sorcerer, one finds such immanent-transcendent inscription in the written spells of French artist and dramatist Antonin Artaud. Setting off on heteroclite pilgrimage from Paris to Ireland's far-flung rocky Oileáin Árann (Aran Islands) in 1937, armed with a magical cane as malefic performance prop and restitution of the ancient crosier of Saint Patrick, Artaud begins his spell-casting activity. A place where Modernity's breakdown between things and words, force and form, has not corroded vitality, the elephant-grey jagged cliffs that halo the island clearly expose vertical and horizontal faults inherent to the bedrock: erosion slices right angles into the flesh of the cliff face, exposing jagged weaknesses like huge cuneiform letters. It is whilst staying with a lighthouse keeper on the scabrous limestone island that Artaud's spell practice is galvanised. Sent in the post a week later, his spell letters were fragile writing papers burned with cigarettes and festooned with magical symbols, alongside darkly humorous letter-writing protocols, to make them immediately acting incantations. Where the graffiti on walls in alehouses and churches draws attention to the place of words inscribed as forms of graffiti, the paper of Artaud's spell could be a microcosmic map of the island itself, where place and surface support fuse, drawing attention, like *Rising Damp*, to the alchemising power of landscape in a metaphysics of materiality that far surpasses pedestrian notions of art and life, and distinctions thereof. The writing becomes the trace of this heretical pilgrimage, and his perambulations across the island's rocky substances.

Artaud's cane, a prop, which disappears upon his arrest in Dublin, fizzing with electricity, as both receiver — through the drilling — and as a transmitter of these forces, seems to be a diabolic radio antenna for the force of the island.[4] The comedy of subversive and contingent slapstick abets this release, as *Rising Damp* does forty years later. More than the material layers of the substrate, which he de(sur)faces with magical protective intent, and more than just the re-made body of Artaud through the fire, the spell, like the Templar whistle in M.R. James's ghost story *Oh Whistle and I'll Come To You My Lad*, is a force to help draw up the "ancient" forces of landscape beyond the scope of the page, or the TV screen. The holes burnt are an intentional piercing into the page to release a force implicit to the magical spell, through a coterminous hole in landscape too, bridging comedy and de(sur)facement at the level of place. To comedically make the present-past re-

---

4   You can't get the staff anymore.

"Return his salutation, marquis — his cane came from the same factory as yours!" Artaud, 1948, and Richie and Eddie from Bottom, *1991.*

emerge, he burns a hole through the present, or, in Artaud's words, he makes "a hole in the world in order to leave it". In 1931, Artaud writes about the power of Dionysian comedy, in relation to the Marx Brothers, film star peers of his, where he finds "the liberation [...] of a particular magic, which the customary relation of words and images does not ordinarily reveal". The drilling of the cane — which is also a pilgrim's staff, sign of the traveller, the "vagabond sign of itinerancy" — underlines the importance of releasing inscription from its pedestrian signification.

Pilgrim banners painted by late Victorian writer "Baron Corvo" or Frederick Rolfe — often signed Fr. Rolfe in shortening and as humorous attempt at clericism — are also insignia of a spiritual geography, related to both a sacred well's myth, and of Rolfe's own philosophical imbrication of art and autobiography. Testament to his infamous itinerancy, they were made during his ill-fated arrival and stay with the Jesuit Fr. Beauclerk at the parochially gaudy Holy Well of St Winefride in North Wales. Rolfe painted them using a technique he claims to have invented — "stained arras" —

arras being the name for a heavy Medieval wall hanging. In blemishing this unprimed canvas, the vaguely naïve modernist gold-leaf scenes of ancient British Saints — also featuring his symbol, the crow, an occult version of *Where's Wally?* — are a mystical production method. The banner images cling to the support, or *subjectile* in Artaud's terms, so that they, once attached to banner poles, can be manhandled through the dwindling industrial valley on the Saint's Day procession.[5] Staining, in Rolfe's case, I think, acts as a de(sur)facement; it is a restitution through thanatological mildew, as though the banners are the rediscovered grave garments of St Winefride herself. Stains appear retroactively, gradually growing, whose legend is the psycho-topography of spiritual symbolism.

William Blake's printmaking methods partake of de(sur) faced aberrancy. Signals in the ancient world being picked up and irradiated through his graver's hands in 1794 (not the 1974 of *Carry On* and *Rising Damp*) whilst he is hard at the furnace in Lambeth, stoking sheets of metal to "reveal the infinite which was hid [already latent]". Etching, a form of intaglio printmaking, where an image is acidically incised into a metal plate using a sharp point, which then holds ink in recessed areas, providing a mirror, or negative to the drawing. Mirror to the fiery pandemonium of technics and the re-surfaced ores of the earth that the Industrial Revolution churned, Blake's etching method, in the melee of the infernal mills, was allegorised in his *Marriage of Heaven and Hell*

---

5   I saw these banners on my own pilgrimage to Holywell: a personal "Quest for Corvo" following A.J.A. Symons' 1934 experiment in biography. Old photos reproduced in early digitisation on county archaeology boards, blotted fabric spectres trailing through the diminutive High Street, haunted the tiny museum.

(c.1790) through the acts of six "chambers", where a "cave", symbolising the copper plate, was made "infinite" and "cast" into the "expanse". This "infernal method" not only envisages though line and form an apocalyptic vision but is a "melting *apparent surfaces* away": an operation of de(sur)facement in which the tension of an individual world is harnessed. Blake's methodology is a self-avowed mythology fusing space and time, borne up from his "Printing house in Hell".

Inscription shown in the spell, the banner, the etching, rank alongside scatological toilet wall daubings and pilgrim's initials as the mystical equivalent of a spiritual path through the microcosmic geography of the surface-support. They open up a continuum, where hieroglyph — *read* as sacred carving — is co-constitutive with the surface it is traced on, and makes a pact with the sediment of place and time. As method-mythology, each iteration engages with a keenly felt "absence" of myth, according to the conditions of access of their world. They materialise time as a stain, galvanised through the embodiment of, and confirmation of the importance of, location and place — both real and imagined.

Noise 4

I heard the residents of Mesopotamia through the Roberts Radio. It was Pentecost Day. Capitalists, newspaper accounts, would-be comic writers... were in the main unconscious of the Manichean playback to which they are listening....

Damp as Time's Patina

"When I decided to publish the script of Rising Damp, my first thought was, did I have them all? What followed was a desperate search in the loft amongst piles of mildewed papers until I found them. They were dog-eared, held together with rusty staples, covered with nicotine stains (I smoked endless panatellas in those days in my search for inspiration), scratchings out and mysterious arrows pointing this way and that, all reflecting the urgency of the time."

This account from the writer of *Rising Damp*, Eric Chappell, locates his scripts in an attic, damp and curling. Damp is an aesthetic experience, as much as index of life's shabby timespans. A nesting of arcane material effects recursively instantiates the theme of the sitcom itself in his description, and self-referentially draws out time from their moment of creation to "now", through the mildewed pulse of duration. As much a timely meditation on the transformation and creative process from writing to broadcast, the patina of the activity upon the colouring pages indicates mystical operations, arrows, scratchings-out like those at Borley Rectory. For Harry Price, these scratches were manifest through the psychic ether: an idea traced through Hermeticism, of a bank of technological memory, known as the Akashic records. These filed banks of curling damp records virtually stored on a plane of occult consistency keep account of time's rupture as a measuring tool for technology, memory and the human.

Traces of inscription from *inhuman* hand are pointers on Chappell's map over and above the words themselves. Damp operates as much as a textual production as the formal text. Damp is the patina of time, but, similarly to *The Stone Tape*, is materially receptive and indurate to linear conceptions of time. Damp as the inscription on a wall functions as an occulted filling system, a mode of recording:

> *MARK E. SMITH: "They say damp records the past: if that's so, I've got the biggest library yet…"* (1984)

The walls of Rigsby's house do not replay the scream of the long-sacrificed, or bear witness to urgent spirits (*"help me"*) but they corroborate Mark. E. Smith's bleak domestic pastoral that the damp in his house is somehow keeping stock of time — is splaying open temporality to a material simultaneity. Smith, lyricist and singer of 1970s Prestwich music group The Fall, shows how, through folk's horror, the power of damp articulates the occulted supernatural squalor of the mundane across materiality of walls sagging heavy with mould: the real occult is on your doorstep. Smith's lyric, from the song "No Bulbs", consequentially, is also about the shitty state of his house — "A light has just gone out/A bulb has just gone out/ No belts in this flat/No bulbs in this flat/In need of white lamp…"

Realigning the hermetic virtual memory bank to a series of mid-Victorian semi-detached houses paints a specifically comic and parochial as much as interdimensional scene for the barely audible yet crucial conclusion to the song, almost muttered as the rockabilly peters out: *They say damp records the past…* It is recording the present too, a cut-up loop that Rigsby's tenants continually bemoan:

> *ALAN: I turn the lights off so she can't see the damp patches.*
> *PHILIP: On you?*
> *ALAN: On the wallpaper!*
> *PHILIP: You might have to turn the lights off completely!*

No lights can hide the damp, or can cover the gap in generations. Post-war houses are recording mediums, rich in 1970s static, but at this period, Smith suggests: "Maybe industrial ghosts are making Spectres redundant". This quality is the strangeness of analogue crackle and incipient neoliberals turn to the apparently "immaterial" labour of globalisation. The texture of life slipping away, grappled with by more contemporary "hauntological" musicians who foreground the auditory quality of ghostly technologies. For Mark Fisher, the "hauntological" trope in this mode connotes an avowed and conspicuous use of crackle, "which renders time as an audible materiality". Such a move, often in reference to such 1970s British artefacts as *The Stone Tape* and other coterminous TV programmes and graphics, recursively labours recorded history's own medium. Fisher's hauntology in part reanimates Jacques Derrida's "*hantologie*" in *Spectres of Marx* as both a spectral ontology of being against linear time and self-identical presence, but also a reflection of Fukuyama's alleged "end of history". The latter, instantiated by the collapse of the hermetic Soviet Empire, as much as the collapse of the dirigiste British Empire state that neoliberalism was gradually affecting. This apparently foretold the disappearance of history in the slipstream of unbridled global capitalism and the resultant "techno-tele-discursivity's" rampant collapsing of space-time. That the 1970s is so utterly redolent in hauntological terms — cue the PIF (public information film) bores — with the potential of grainy artefacts to hallucinate a revised view of it in the present, is surely down to the disturbing effects channelled through visual culture of the period. This is a phase shift into the post-industrial, intensified and beached up on the shores of creaking Victorian infrastructure.

The short time span is a feedback loop of autophagous reference, which damp as medium and metaphor attempts corrosion of, preforming the incursion of the ancient. Where tape crackle is an auditory historicism and mediumistic interpretation through the archaeology of haunting, damp vies to be time's visual materialisation. Damp as an arcane script renders time a visual materiality, as much as analogue audio materialises audio history's layering. In refence to the ITV and BBC sitcom, it locates a particularly British and (at times) public broadcasting service — it eschews the former's nostalgia mode through its century-spanning reach, functioning in the mode of the epiphanous *Stone Tape* rather than as paratextual refence thereto.

Damp's transtemporality is disarranging timescales through simultaneous recording and storing. Also a material model of decay for the sitcom's house: a graffiti-heavy yet inhuman form of defacement that is also an individuated production. To this hieroglyphic: both the misery of Rigsby's torrid life and the hauntological ghost of Britain's neoliberalism, and further, a sewage works and slag heap spectre hovering in magical de(sur)facement. (N.B. it goes without saying that The Fall's LP *Hex Enduction Hour* (1982) is an ultra de(sur) facement of the vinyl sleeve). Such a stain writes that England is in decay, and that Rigsby's tenement is falling down, but that in its very temporal heaviness, it escapes being indexed solely though hauntology, whose techno-tele-discursivity is predated by damp. A psychogeographic modality to profanely sacralise space-time in effervescent blooms of green and black, as an inhuman *writing on the wall* of ancient presence, an inconvenient rem(a)inder of not just the torrid, but of *time itself* — as much a biblical refence highlighting a sacred currency to the archaeological trace, as to the technological formation, via primal mud and clay, and squalid disconsolation, of our souls, post-Fall (and The Fall). Faith is a necessary player in this. Its shadows leave faint singes on the skin, ritual burn marks echoed in the archaeological disruption of time's enclosure. These technological crop marks are there: time ghosts all successive technologies, despite the internet's collapsing of both space and time.[6] If hauntology was a resistance to this homogenisation, it will be next to examine how ancient systems of writing pre-empt and irrigate these and other bleak landscapes of historicism, to instantiate a heavily BC stain on a continuum that links television as a medium to the marshland's post-Fall babble.

---

6   Premature memorialising cannot replace the office of the soul.

Noise 5

The decal of Holsten nostalgia is crushed on the pavement, after a journey from inebriated export to the English mustard and green bile... It's the original Fabricke of transport... I felt like a Brewing company Rep, but extremely BC.

Cuneiform

The Odd Lager

Holsten Pils, in its erstwhile position as the original beer import, brings together British dissolution and ancient resonance as damp comestible. *Code: Damp*'s curling records are unfolding a weird dynamic: the 1970s, the tenancy and damp. Or, time, place and de(sur)facement. In thinking about how to surreally manifest these weighty contingencies, I translated, with the help of Prof. Irving Finkel, philologist and chief curator of the Middle East at the British Museum, the old Holsten Pils advert tagline *The Odd Lager* into the ancient text of cuneiform, the Earth's oldest known script system.

Of course, no *direct* translation from this Archē scriptwriting into Roman advertising semantics can be made, but in this

The Odd Lager.

meeting of meaning systems, a folk horror of the beer industry distilled something about technology's transformational powers. In the marshes, this retroactive Archē writing has unfolded: a pre-cognition of the role of writing as the invention of externalised memory surface. Speech is at once hardened into marsh mud yet abstracted through inscribed pattern, beginning the record of a territorial timestamp that decries the priority of the given over the made.

A blurring of timelines at the level of materiality's damp occurred here. Cuneiform is a technic inscribed upon clay, emerging from the Mesopotamian floodplains, an alluvial salt marsh — between the Tigris and Euphrates rivers, which once circumnavigated the ancient ruins of Ur and Uruk — which is now the south and southeastern reaches of Iraq.[1] It's from the spiky perpendicular figures, serendipitous incisions made by marsh water reeds onto marsh clay, that gives it the name, from the Latin "*cuneus*", meaning "wedge". From this germinating and multiply-hexed territory, traces were formed: handfuls of the clay moulded into brick writing tablets, removed or *de-territorialised* from the mud, and enfolded into a process of human memory, in the first "known" writing.

Derrida had, in the 1970s, as *Rising Damp* was broadcast and Holsten poured, made the point that writing as the trace or *trait* — functioning like the spectre of *hantologie* — wasn't just scratched into a substrate but was the differential play of dissolving traces dependent on a context, never entirely present, but traced through that which is exterior to it, and to the hand of its author, long passed. Always referring

---

1   "Arise upon thy Watches let us see thy Globe of fire/On Albions Rocks
    & let thy voice be heard upon Euphrates" Blake, *Jerusalem*, plate 84.

to that outside of itself, a haunting presence within text: a con-text. The cuneiform's wrenching out of con-text is an intense moment of memory's industrialisation, read as a disappearance of place, of the specificity of a locality.

In these Akkadian glyphs of cuneiform, a beer's tagline is charged into a sigil-like spell: the first document of history. If folk horror is the reckoning of landscapes to the pains of modernity, Holsten as ancient drink is its libation to the rusting shop sign: dissolution in a can, a ludic tincture for re-entry into the present, which is to say, re-entry into how we understand time through technology.[2] Holsten in this case is also a technology, or a "desiring machine". Notwithstanding the fact that the earliest beer production is dated to this period of the Sumerians, around 4000BC, evidenced in a tablet excavated in Mesopotamia that showed parishioners drinking a beverage from a bowl with straws.

Cuneiform emblematises the disruption of existence, and the beginning of an industrialised historicity because it is the point where prehistory stops and history begins, the original archaeo-industrialisation through incised glyphs: where the notion of time as a recorded material instantiates itself.[3] With each incision of the reed onto the clay, a web of access points to and in time is charted. This is as if to say that the letters were emerging from the clay, but also a graffitiing back behind the veil to *see* the scriptural "ground" of mud, according a modern plasticity of space to ancient mud as writing's time travel.

---

2   "The esoteric language is the technical language" — *The Morning of the Magicians.*

3   "They say damp records the past."

Seeing is key, as history is a tele-*vision*, a seeing-far, a divination. This makes the sitcom, too, readable as an electronic vision, a tele-vision event, of more ancient history. Recorded history is the condition of time. Cuneiform writing is the real substate of the TV, and in so being, relocates the hauntological crisis of recent historicity into a marshy medium. Technics are haunted from these ancient marsh landscapes, with damp the

Marshy Medium.

magical material linking the simultaneous event palimpsest from landscape to Rigsby's house.

The damp hieroglyphics of Rigsby's walls domesticates text as "an assemblage of textures into which memory has been woven", as Bernard Stiegler describes inscription. *Rising Damp* disavows the rarefied scriptures of deconstruction for a humorously weird living condition though: a domestic anachronism that allows the walls to extend space into time. Abetted by spilt Holsten Pils, left to soak into the floor near the radiator.

Bernard Stiegler's metaphysics of reality structured by such technics has run this Promethean force, marking the start of a form of "history" as that moment at which memory is given form in Mesopotamia: an exteriorisation, from the cuneiform through to the tape machine and digital communications. Not just a means to an end, not just instrumentalisation, but the double-edged sword of existence, implicit to any understanding of time as constitutive of the human, as a giving and taking of territory. This makes the cuneiform tablet as much an index of "capitalism" as the marsh. The earliest scripts betray the legend of accountancy, with the oldest cuneiform tablets, as Jean Bottéro concurs, "simple mnemotechnical devices [...as] lists" for hop keeping [for beer], livestock and other admin necessities. The ploughing of a furrow and the line of writing are analogous, the farming machinery shaping the topology of thought and site, in a pharmakonic gesture — Holsten as poison and antidote, hallucinogen and rapture. The pharmakon, as Stiegler explains in *What Makes Life Worth Living*, designates that which is "at once what enables care to be taken and that of which care must be taken...its power is curative to the immeasurable extent that it is also destructive". Two sides of the same coin. How right De Vere-Brown was, in the "political" episode of *Rising Damp*, to insist that damp was the "unacceptable face of capitalism"! A Janus-headed (sur)face, comodulating the accelerated sphere of technics that devours space in favour of commercially driven time that contracts place's ability to haunt, but which has its genesis in the arcane swamp of conditioning. Hard Pils to swallow, but

Beer and deep time: two sides of the same coin…

whose prescription to both strangeness and infrequency (*Odd*) is this experience of time in dampness.

Marsh Cut-Up

Time is charted across the surface of the tablet, a *tele*-vision of time seen in a delimited surface area. Not only does this tether mud clay to the genesis writing, but imbricates both within a specific landscape of the marsh.

Damp marsh clay, from which this *Ur*-moment of history comes, *is* the medium of time, the way in which time appears as space. We had already assumed this through more prosaic British quarters: like the force-form of Rigsby's walls re-surfacing the strange material depth of time spent in the late mid-century. The depth of the "field" in both senses is unfathomable deep, and its weird stratigraphy funnels down to what Alan Garner terms that "deep connection with the land, which doesn't stop at ground level. A ploughed field is not a ploughed field; it goes down and down and down in space and time, but into timelessness, not linear time but cyclical time."

A movement from perceived "Flat Time" to the supernatural depths of marsh time might only be revealed only through modes of supernatural archaeology. The cuneiform tablet as a symbol and an object of this transit from marsh to human interpretation, a Mud Flat Time, which tethers technological advances of writing (and printing press, computers) to both place but also the spatio-temporality of haunting — on the premise that haunting itself involved a spatialisation of a different time, a presence of absence. Haunting as a key mode of the twentieth century collapses globalisation's speedy flattening of space-time. This is not just as hallucination, but also as a retroactive revelation of how these elements function in respect of the mythic.

The mythic as methodology — as seen in Artaud, Rolfe and Blake — rather than being a developmental conceptual scaffolding, is implicit to this magico-materiality of damp as the spatialisation of time. It is from the alchemising power of the landscape that damp, as materiality's historicity, is distilled. In historical terms, this could be seen in the alchemist's collection of morning "dew" from early morning water vapour on cloths that have been left out: skilful harvesting by hands used to spagyric work, for the collection of universal energies from the land that will be put through various processes of distillation to reach the metaphoric "gold" through the materials of the earth. Writing surfaces, too, collect the damp. The marsh, the "damp part of the world", is the Archē substratum from which material metaphysics seeps. Earmarked for what Denis Hollier terms its "resistance to system and homogeneity", Georges Bataille's theorisation of certain materiality in base matter can, like the hermeneutical and textual sediment of the marsh, when matched with a depth of geological *différance* (the spatialisation of time), "re-stimulate ancient association" and indeed re-channel the mythic as this methodology. Base matter in its move from high ideal to lowly excreta, brings mud, amongst other things, into a mythic plane. It makes the marsh an energy field of history: a terrain allowing an occult contraption of time travel.

With such time-travel, that base matter as a powerful force and process, the cartography indexed in the tablet, occurs here between virtual marsh sites: ancient Mesopotamia has parity to contemporary marshes — the grim Essex version buzzes with a squalid forcefield, in its valorising of the "much-maligned" county of wastelands. They interface epistemes of changing technology, meteorology and temporality, manifest from the thick mud and the mist of its constitution, that disorient the marsh's inhibitor: added to the water that drains, seeps, steeps therein.

Marshes are anterior zones, "magic circles", whose boundaries are not clearly delimited, but rather, fractal,[4] recursive: the repetitive scales of the shore, its cursory boundary, attesting more to what philosopher of the occult Eugene Thacker would call a magic circle's "dark inverse": an anonymous manifestation of an opaque modality that its damps and mists — in the Essex marsh variant — are a weird metonymy to.

Damp was always there in the cuneiform's function, making the small temporal surfaces of clay, like Artaud's spells, into

---

4   Appropriately, the term "fractal" was coined by mathematician Benoît Mandelbrot, who posed the thought experiment "How Long is the Coastline of England?" in a 1967 paper. The term comes from the Latin world Latin word *fractus* ("fragmented" or "broken").

hardened maps of alchemical landscapes The magical-materialist conception of the damp permits this temporal strangeness, a border-material permitting transit between epochs emblematised in the movement cyphered in ground and figure, between clay and cuneiform mark.

The marsh landscape is the originary symbolic zone, but finds in the walls of the house an analogue, bringing the sacred geography of pilgrimage to de(sur)face the boundary of the walls (as much as the threshold moment of the 1970s), whilst also retrospectively filing it in the ledger of virtual psychic formation: a formation founded on the memory — or its externalisation — implicit in writing's purpose. The abysmal support abets a formation of the subject, setting its rhythms loose in the face of symbolic misery, where algorithmic-driven commerce substitutes temporal experience.

RIGSBY: It's an old house. You don't know what these walls have seen.

The walls have seen time — a tele-visual mode apposite to the technological medium they are appearing in. But the transmutation between muddy material and inscribed abstraction as de(sur)facement that instantiates human symbolic thought is arguably also mythologised in The Fall of biblical proportions (and shimmering affectively through the Camus novel and the British music group of the same name). Rigsby, in transmuting the damp base matter of life into meaningful model, achieves a gnosis relative to this renewed yet perhaps bombastic sense of being. Transmutation in alchemy prioritises both the physical acceleration of material turning to gold, as much as it is a material processual metaphor for spiritual fulfilment, in undoing the supposed ravages of the Fall. A spiritual schism metaphorically represented by the advent of writing in the alchemical landscape of the marsh from the muddy ground of reality as material, elemental, constantly transformative, and impersonal.

The alienation of the Fall also engenders an ignominious elation of fracture, push and pull between territory and its loss, between orientation and its inverse: disorientation. A purposive form to the "originary rift", which in turn occasions the grot, the baseness. For *Naturphilosoph* Friedrich Schelling, life out of this swamp of alienation, or one at least elevated from the "ground", is necessarily contaminated, full of restlessness and decay. Damp is a validation of squalid yet sacred materiality as a rhetoric of corruption (a contagion that will be a modality later of the Essex marshes themselves). For Schelling, this dissonance of spirit is, also, the cause of a deterritorialisation, a disorienting of the spirit, but one that rests, for Schelling, on an inversion of high and low. The germ of an earthy curse, a metastable evil of the human. By contrast, the disorienting Babel of ancient Mesopotamia, and the fragmentation within language — in fact, everything post-Eden — is a more joyous impure dissipation, with fragmented sherds of millennia-old cuneiform brick: "you are handling, as it were, the materials and processes of delirium", says William Burroughs.

Everything pre-Eden, then, is also delirious. Jean-François Lyotard, writing in 1974 — perhaps let's call it Anno Damp, *AD 74*, the year *Rising Damp* first aired — added that people enjoy the anonymity of the pub and the suburb as originary dissonance, because "there has never been nor ever will be such a body bound up in its unity and identity, that this body is a phantasy". The spatial vagaries and time-travel of the cuneiform are destabilising a clear duality between the absolute language of technics and mystical practices, and likewise, between originary and soiled, between myth and science. In hermeticism's "occult science", a speculative and syncretic collage of knowledge validates this method, both before and after the Enlightenment distinction of empiricism with mythic fear, and of the capitalist subject with a notion of Edenic purity.

As shadowy parallel to modernity, hermeticism's syncretic approach inhabits the threshold zone of knowing and unknowing, playing with a line of fracture between legibility and strangeness. This scabrous line cohering a bricolage of marsh effects is formally echoed in the fractal ruinous edge of the fragment, given that most writing tablets are found in a broken or incomplete state. The scabrous edge of the tablet predetermines us to see the past as broken, ruined, much as the wiping of BBC tape recordings occults memory of certain periods. Where the fractal edge of the tablet is a fractal map of its marsh coastline, it's brokenness also reflects the deracination of landscape: the writing of memory is always the implementation of a montage of "cut" and "paste", basic concepts for digital text processing, as much as the cuneiform.

RIGSBY: [during a séance] You think I'm going to be fooled by that? You've got a tape recorder behind there!

In the face of the cuneiform's stuttering of recorded time, the neoliberal "end of history" starts to take on a pallid hue. If technics, when seen as a regime of progress, is a flattening of the marsh myth, a Holsten hauntology of the cuneiform tablet reveals that damp records the past and more importantly, a magical damp regime that corrodes any certitude thereof, by showing that landscape *itself* is the original fragmented disoriented writing script: a proto-cut-up, whose affect is to disarticulate a flattening sense of temporality. A marshy substratum that is at once archaic *and* modern, with the incision into the marsh clay as the knife-edge cut into alienation: a surgical severance of the psyche from imbrication in the "natural". Damp's simultaneous recording and cutting up eschews hauntological fatalistic time. Burroughs recalls: "events are pre-written and pre-recorded and when you cut words, lines, the future leaks out". You always have the whole of Earth history under your feet, so to speak, palpitating in mud, in wells, in walls, *sous les pavés*.

Television is a radical cutting, because it cuts up images into current, before its reassembly in the consumer electronic. In spooling the remains of a TV video on which the studio sitcom was recorded, you plummet the depths of time, of cut-up historical spatiality, swirling down not just the recorded timestamps but the stratigraphy of marsh mythography. The crackle and hiss of the rewind sound searching for disruption on the archaeological record. The Maxell C90 bears this legend, recording in its magnetic dust the code from Mesopotamia. The *Ur*-technology in more ways than one, the dissipative Essex marsh script is alive and well in such recent juddering tape technology, proof of damp's de(sur)facing modality, written in muddy opacity, through the passages of historiographical mutation.

Adam Bohman, current tape collagist of Catford, engages in a constant form of this production, creating C90 travel cassettes that record a bricolage of texts seen in various forms on the journey (adverts, train stops, shop signs), sounds heard, and sights seen, in magnetic tape as parity: "Damp Window Logic", as the sonic drayman reads on his "trip tape" to Sheerness. This humorous methodology is a laughter track in the tracks made through a place, in the joyous dis/orientation of spatialising time. A unique combination of tape and journey at one with the methodology of the Mesopotamian *Ur*-tape.[5] You are not simply rewinding the occult contraption of the tape, but also intervening in the time of the Mesopotamian and Essex marsh through the process of playback. Uncovering, thereby, the artefacts of the damp electromagnetic memory process itself: strange temporality in sediment as figure to the ground of the tape strip. Derrida's *trait* as the "spatialisation of time — the "becoming-space of time" is, due to the tape's unique analogue material capacities, purposeful in re-editing site itself. Finger, button, switch, play, rewind, producing it again (and again and again) as a difference. An enchantment this is a practice of tape pilgrimage to re-edit the marsh's

UR-tape: Live from Mesopotamia — "great for everyday recording".

---

5   Cf. *Nuncio Ref!* cassette, Leonard Rossiter's Lost Mystery Play

spatio-temporality by retroactive insertion into the past unearths shallower disturbances. TV plays are received into the popular memory according to their fate at the wiper's hands. A distinctly unsentimental immediacy of recycling that is the doom of many spectral lost broadcasts. Damp, both located in the marsh and seeping into all aspects of life, reels forwards and backwards in time, only becoming injurious when the place-markers of the sacred (the marsh) mutate into flat specular metaphor.

A "proto-collage" or cut-up method was prevalent amongst Mesopotamian scribes, who reburied cuneiform tablets differing in age and provenance by some 2,000 years: when they unearthed ancient inscriptions and then re-buried them as time capsules inside building foundations with contemporary equivalents, performing defacement as production through digging and rearranging blocks of text, they reveal a new reality that was there all along. This finds yet more dubious purchase in *Carry On Up the Khyber* (1968), a colonial satire that finds gauche joy in the absurd political campaigns within Iraq and Afghanistan's marshes and soil: perhaps proof that, because and despite the eviscerating embarrassment of British attitudes and establishment humour, something heterogeneous still flickers in that land.[6] It is reverberating out of Iraq, the centre of focus in the War on Terror and the wider Middle East, as implicated in a neoliberal corporate economics grounded in oil, that affirmation of the fractal cut-up's call to the future, persists. Irving Finkel has suggested that, despite the devastation at humanitarian and

6   BBC documentary *Bitter Lake* (2015), directed and written by Adam
     Curtis, featured cut-up sequence from this *Carry On* film in his extended
     essay on the centuries-long campaigns in Afghanistan.

archaeological levels through the invasion of Iraq in the early 2000s, untold numbers of cuneiform tablets are still dormant: sleeper agents in the earth. Iraq then becomes one iteration of Burroughs's "Interzone" where writing machines come alive in a reportage-fantasy purgatory of the ever-written Middle East, a fictioning no less true to the fractious embellishments of national histories and myth transmitted via generations of transductive devices.

Cuneiform's status in very recent years has also changed amongst the current population of "Mesopotamia" in their celebration of one hundred years as a nation state, founded by the British mandate. Archaeology plays a role in this new nation's consciousness, underlined by the founding of the Iraq Museum in 1926: a legitimacy that is based on both a Mesopotamian and Islamic state. Interest in cuneiform now

Car Park Hermeneutics.

satisfies a demand for ideas of international regionalism, which has made it an import signifier of identity since 1921.

One of the largest pieces of graffiti in the world, by a young Iraqi artist known as "Osama Art", says "peace" in Arabic, using cuneiform wedge shapes: an ancient enlargement in the heart of the zone, located on the roof of Al-Sinak garage in Baghdad. At a size of 22 × 4 meters, seeing it in completion requires an air drone, such as those used for militarised warfare and bomb strikes. Graffiti meets a car park in the heart of fractal text, in Baghdad, already underwritten by destructive conflict.[7]

> *BURROUGHS: The Word is divided into units which be all in one piece and should be so taken, but the pieces can be had in any order being tied up back and forth, in and out and fore and aft like an innaresting sex arrangement.*

Modes jostle diachronically from tape to digital in the virtual cyber-pilgrimage mediating much of the marsh bricolage, finding some parity in the contemporary's nonexclusively of site. Such syncopated layers of ancient, early Modern, Modern, Modernity is an enactment more apposite to a "globalised" series of flows. Fast shifts in landscape and

---

7   The identifiers of extremist organisations run to murder and mutilation as signalling characters in digital propaganda: in this line of thinking, artist Om Lekha — citing Middle East reporter Robert Fisk's anecdote of a human body during the Iraq insurgency appearing at a mortuary with a dog's head sewn to the severed neck — describes the "Anubis encounter" qua warfare mutilation of a corpse as a "digital-era hieroglyph"

the traversal of space in faster time. Damp articulates and disavows the globalised practice of fast flows by predating not just the flow of hyperindustrial infotainment, and affect, but the carving of that channel. A channel both riverine, a carving out of estuary mud, but a carving coterminous with its sitcom hermeneutics in the human. In the new meet-up of natural sciences, Damp's Code runs the switchboard for new information and distributed digital feedback loops. Across vast tracts of Essex mudflat are the damp scripts records that c(r)ackle with a malefic charge. This prosody dug from the bogs mutates landscape into technology. The result? Handfuls of clay scooped up from the Essex marshes really do contain cuneiform letters.

Noise 6

Van Der Graaf lyrics wallpaper the pavement, credits discarded, as is their wont... I'm getting mashed to Guillaume de Machaut.

Technology is a Form of Obliteration

(WC) Pan

Television is a mode of "obliteration", according to Richard Dyer's *Light Entertainment*, written in 1973 for the *BFI Television Monograph* series. When *Rising Damp* was just coming into Chappell's consciousness, Dyer describes the "sheer ghastliness" of thousands of TV aerials (or marsh reeds) over Northern Britain's terraced roads: "antennae reaching for escape to another world". Key in the benevolent scheduler's arsenal was the awareness of the "stresses of work and life"

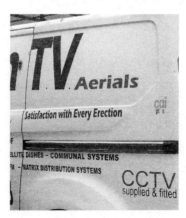

Sheer ghastliness.

in post-industrial societies, for which Light Entertainment and comedy, on occasion, acted as a palliative.

Rising Damp already assumes an "aesthetics of escape", but it is conjoined with the implicit joyous necessity of escape in the first place. Whilst damp and its attendant metaphysic might unsettle the evening viewing, such crawling presence is an inarticulate yet fulsome lectionary of escape itself, aligning ancient landscapes, and the sitcom, with damp as a temporal de(sur)facement of time. Incidentally, Lyotard insists, in *AD 1974*, that industrial subjects are still at liberty to "enjoy swallowing the shit of capital, its materials, its metal bars, its polystyrene, its books, its sausage pâtés, swallowing tonnes of it till you burst".

Media studies has a drab inability to come to terms with this very idea that pleasure might in itself be important, and not just a tool of satiation. The "positive thinking", as imperatives of entertainment founder with damp, as Rigsby mutters from the prayer sheet of marsh hymns, whose torrid domesticity and lurking fear parallel Britain's esoteric tradition. Films like *Blood on Satan's Claw* or the claustrophobic BBC TV programme *Robin Redbreast* from 1970 (another *Play for Today*) that twin contemporary themes of the "permissive society" with disrupted archaeology, rural fertility sacrifice and the antisocial behaviour of bespectacled antiquarians, urges — what would an archaeology episode consist of? *Quatermass* meets *Rising Damp*: Rigsby discovers an ancient Roman ruin in the basement of the house, to remind us all that base matter is the foundation of modernity.[1] Craven smiles and grotesque faces formed out the lichen are more horrific

---

1   Anthony Aloysius Hancock refuses to play the blobs of green matter in *Quatermass* in a 1959 episode of *Hancock's Half Hour*. "Its Hob's Lane all over again!"

with a laughter track — a backing track of more-than-dead audience members, to match the very live studio audience that all episodes were played out in front of — in Yorkshire Television's Kirkstall Road Leeds Studio.

The archaeological record here requires a more ludic excavation method. Disruption in the layers of geological record is like noise from the TV. Scraping the trowel on the East Anglian crown in the marshes sounds a disruption of time. The spectacle-churning addictions of the hyper digital can't compete with such delirious layers, but can add narrative material to its consequences.

PAXTON: You remember me telling you I was interested in archaeology…

Arthur Machen's proto-psychogeographic writings based in both Wales and London proved him to be a seeker of landscape's hidden language, conjuring the Romanesque ruin of the fortress of Isca Silurum in *The Hill of Dreams* (1907) beset with the dark materials of crawling fungus, its deliquescent putrescence coterminous across centuries with modern life trapped in the primeval sludge of its own becoming. Suburban houses founded on "brickfields" whose legends may be the garbled post-script of some Akkadian edict…

> "Nothing exquisite, it seemed, could exist in the weltering suburban sea, in the habitations which had risen from the stench and slime of the brickfields. It was as if the sickening fumes that steamed from the burning bricks had been sublimed into the shape of houses, and those who lived in these grey places could also claim kinship with the putrid mud."

79

Machen proves that the torrid *mise-en-scène* of modernity is matched by a more-than-dead magical material that is its legend and undoing.[2]

As well as the inscription of the living onto the external non-living — damp makes text living, or further, takes the import of humanity's central life from its pedestal. The creeping green marks on the wall or the inscriptions of the cuneiform marks are spatio-temporalised as the medium of history, as both a form and disorienting force. Both human and damp are other than themselves: host to, and of, shadows. Pouring disdain on limited conceptions of self that don't bow to the cumulative melee of time's anachronistic inscription, undermining and overmining our anthropomorphic understanding of phenomena through the un-dead c.r.e.e.p of damp, the human corrals with energies that are not its own. Machen's wan protagonist, Lucian, intuits this: "No doubt, the damp was rising, and the odour of the earth filled the house, and made such as entered draw back, foreseeing the hour of death."

Reason enough for mitigating the "sheer ghastliness" of such grey moments, is found in "Fire & Brimstone", when the Welsh missionary Gwyn, with bulbous rolling eyes, calls down the wrath of the Almighty as Rigsby sits in in pinstripe jacket over the remains of a fish and chip supper. The musty Evangelic incites thunder and lightning as Reggie leaps around the Sarsons: a quotidian ghoulishness,

---

2   In Robert Aickman's *The Stains* (1980) an unspecified form of green lichen appears to grow on protagonist Stephen, his unearthly partner, and eventually his office and house walls, which he abandons to entropy. Damp here is an atavistic colonisation, a weird mirror of the colonisation of life by the commodity form.

a grotesque realism, all the more pungent for its weird admixture of vast metaphysical desolation and British spookiness. Calling on him to repent, as well as to not go through with the wedding and East Anglian honeymoon, a greasy ritual exhuming a self-determined path within the sediment of the house.

(WC) Pan books.

MISSIONARY GWYN: I've saved her [Miss Jones] *from a lifetime of regret, and you from that place of unceasing turmoil.*
RIGSBY: What are you talking about? You've never even been to Yarmouth.

Escape isn't always pretty, and quite often comes, as with the popularity of horror as a genre, through the ravages of the industrial revolution, for which Frankenstein and Dracula vie as the legends. Enjoyable dissolution speaks to the popularity of the *Hammer* franchise and folk horror, at this time, as the cannibalistic feast of a crappy Jack the Ripper

Victoriana, which Rigsby voraciously devours, despite it terrifying him.

RIGSBY: *I can see all the films I want to see on the television...* Dracula, Bride of Dracula, Frankenstein and the Monster [...] *I've seen* The Mummy's Hand *as well. These films are very educational.*

ALAN: *Oh, yes, if you want to know how to kill a vampire, or hold a black mass, or invoke the devil.*

RIGSBY: *As a matter of fact, these films are a manifestation of the eternal struggle between good and evil — revealing the darker side of human nature.*

The funnelling of pre-Enlightenment Hermeticism finds its mid-century terminus in pulp Pan Horror books. Pan in the bullrushes, and on the bookshelves. Late Industrial Revolution-period occult groups, like the Hermetic Order of the Golden Dawn, through to the mid-war wicca boom and the gradual authentication of various "alternative" beliefs shored up as viable alternatives to monotheistic systems, is "mythic fear turned radical". Pulp paperbacks by Dennis Wheatley transformed Crowley-esque sexual and ritual practices into even more gauche popular thrillers for the reading public of the post-war years — stories that themselves became part of the brittle exploitation end of occult cinema in the 1960s.

Wheatley's most famous paperback, *The Devil Rides Out* (1934), was adapted in Terence Fisher's 1968 film of the same name with Christopher Lee, and follows naff upper-class types mortally loafing with a satanist group. The sediment of the film came into Essex reporter purview when I interviewed actor Leon Greene, at his home located just five minutes from my grandfather's house, about his role as Rex in *Devil*, alongside his more famous acting counterpart. Suburban Eastwood reminiscences of his part as Prodigius in the TV film *Further Up Pompeii!* alongside the sweet-naturedly paranoid Frankie Howerd — "*Funny* bloke. He used to think there were space men up above, looking at the Earth and watching over us" — to hell-raising from Oliver Reed, underlines the comedy of his celebrity patina, and the imposing Rex van Ryn role: evident in a flash of Hammer in his domestic bliss, sitting outside his suburban house called The Forum — the deeds for which, he said, had been witnessed by John Pertwee.

If the horror films are the dark truth of 1970s folks, they recursively double now as set-pieces decaled with nostalgia. *Rising Damp*'s transmutation of the mundane into the marvellous is precisely a side-step into the arena of *comedy* as oddness (why add horror to folk?) that Arthur Machen maintained existed alongside beauty as a legitimate mode of art. Despite his *ennui* and disgust at the state of the industrial, Machen permitted egress in the built-up metropolis, as much as the damp and oozing grottos of his homeland. With this in mind, *Rising Damp* is not an updated and rarefied lifestyle Paganism with attendant accessories. With *Rising Damp*, the spagyric oozing of life as irreverent and disturbing oscillates around the grains of a duality of humour and the hermetic. Machen's short stories and novels, all of which detail a late decadent atmosphere of mysticism seeping into the twentieth century, examine this tension between the material and the idea, a materialist mysticism, where the fabric of the present can be magically purposive. This colliding of the numinous within the empirical, which for him happens at sites of Pagan intensities — the shade of groves, the summits of mountains, the dense grotesque and hallucinatory forms made of forest vegetation — is in the sitcom occurring at the threshold of the walls. Both instances are thin places of transit, making the sitcom another portal to the numinous.

Machen shows that the spagyric — or damp — element is necessary to the domestic, in as much as it might channel down to the primal depths and unnerve the fabric of the everyday, and in so doing helps underline *Rising Damp*'s collision of mundanity and terror. This fiction bespeaks the incomprehensible and horrific, with a comic framing afforded by the sitcom which inheres most in the mode of the comically grotesque, the carnivalesque, or "grotesque realism", as Bakhtin described its Medieval form. The grotesque, a Romanesque collage of human and unhuman effects, is also a comic metaphysics, if this is a way of plunging into the fantastical through the mundane that doesn't aestheticise the past but makes of it a vital reconfiguration — through the framing of a popular, perhaps ghastly, forms of inhuman genesis. Writing on French seventeenth-century writers Rabelais and Béroalde, outlining a mode of "Pantagruelism", named after one of the titular giants in Rabelais's ribald and satiric *Gargantua and Pantagruel* (c. 1532), the grotesque, ribald and carnivalesque romances are representation of manifold concealed and wonderful mysteries, and point, for Machen, to the "harlequinade" of humanity. He goes on: "The Harlequin was a man to whom it had been given to see and understand the *laughter* that lies everywhere hidden" — waiting in the damp that creeps up walls, or as Machen has it, "the fire lies hidden in the flints and stones".

Seeing Rigsby as a "type" of Machen's Harlequin demonstrates the same inherent physical agility in his jumpy backward gait, his trickster qualities, as a supernatural creation. The Harlequin itself stems from a Devil in the popular medieval mystery plays, the most well-known medieval cycles of which were from York, Coventry, Chester, Lincoln and East Anglia. All were performed by guilds: "In York, Mystery Plays dramatised the Bible from the Fall of Man (performed by the Coopers) to the Last Judgement (performed by the Mercers). As part of the cycle, the Flood was performed by the Fishers and Mariners, the Slaughter of the Innocents by the Girdlers and Nailers and the Resurrection by the Carpenters." Official professional communities sanctioned by a form of technological commerce tied to cosmic schema,[3] the mystery play, rolling through Britain on wagons, is the medieval repertory theatre that was many later drama actors' trades. The repetition of a rote set of performances, toured across parishes, was the entertainment of the day, and *Rising Damp* — which incidentally itself began life as a play, *The Banana Box*, with all but Richard Beckinsale and Rossiter in place (*Steptoe*'s Wilfred Brambell played Rigsby) — could be a mystery play, with Rossiter as Machiavellian trickster.

ERIC CHAPPELL: You can tell that Rising Damp *is by a frustrated theatre writer. All the action could take place on a stage.*

The travelling mystery play pageant wagon is revised as a form in *Damp*'s recording studio. But this is also a past captured by microphones and camera. Perhaps, though, this not simply rewinding the occult contraption of the tape, but also intervening in the time of the *marsh* through the process of TV

---

3   The revival of mystery plays, particularly the Chester mystery plays
     in the 1970, recreated not only the cyclic nature of the plays, but also
     the processional staging of them along medieval festival routes and
     the use of wagons designed on existing descriptions of their medieval
     counterparts.

playback. In recording the past, damp simultaneously edits or interferes with it too, as it does the cuneiform's heritage.

The pop culture medium of the sitcom's genesis is music hall, through an incipient form of television as a broadcast media, following the development of film and movie image. Music hall relied on a humorous destructiveness and not narrative, a string of patter unbound by linear structure. Despite being the basis for the broadcast sitcom, the latter serial form of broadcasting required the tropes of characterisation, narrative and repetitive allusion. This electronic substitute for collective experience is TV's video approximation of theatre, an attempt at the live play experience through the then live laughter of the recorded laugh track.

Rising Damp as a sitcom doesn't stray far from traditional genre expectations in terms of structure and style, and the counterpoint of each character's relationship is neatly meted out with the sympathetic torsions of performance. *Rising Damp* looks like a sitcom: filmed in the proscenium arch, bright lights, in front of a live Leeds audience. Later breakdowns of this set-up, from docu-fiction, and fast edits, are symptoms of their time and are largely an embourgeoisement of television comedy, which never really tore down the fourth wall — with the possible exception of *The Young One*'s Vivian ripping down, or de(sur)facing, the opening credits to *The Good Life*.[4] The archetypal *popular* form is exactly the place for the ingress of the weird mystery play. Despite damp being the medium of history, the idea that old-fashioned British humour subsists through a dampening weight of bathos is only half

---

4   The destructive *affischiste* tendency extends to Situationist posters papering *The Young Ones'* kitchen.

Bad Life.

the story. Damp is the undermining of common sense, the incompleteness of each moment.

Rising Damp is excused from disassembling the models of TV broadcasting. Its metaphysics lies in the rigid structure that allows the damp to seep through. Lurid imaginings hinted at in occasional anti-naturalism, in the marsh landscape that the characters swim through, narrativised instead by the demonic speed of both Rigsby's speech and the speed of the frantic production itself.

This filming was an endless rota: "Shows had to be written in a fortnight, rehearsed in a week, recorded in an hour and a half, and put out in twenty-five minutes, and then the process repeated all over again." Industrial light entertainment production for commercial expediency to keep the masses mollified, but also necessary electrical charge, these endlessly repeated movements make a stain on the TV glass: a set of physical coordinates that might tear Rigsby out of camera shot and into the living room. Four years before *The Stone Tape*, Nigel Kneale's 1968 *The Year of the Sex Olympics* tarried with mid-century entertainment as necessary opiate, combining the occult technical topography of his *Stone Tape* with the incipient rise of "reality TV". Society is divided into "low drives" and "high drives". The former are pacified with constant pornography broadcasts, but a live calamity suggests to TV coordinator Ugo Priest — played by Leonard Rossiter (!) — the potential of a new entertainment concept, and his new show *The Live-Life Show* is born. The horror of reality TV is abetted by humour, helped of course by Rossiter: or as Nigel Kneale said himself of M.R. James's stories, *dry humour heightening the frightful*. Rossiter's ghosting of Nigel Kneale progs, as a priest of technological Modernity, transcends the TV Plays into the wider sacred theatre of the period. Rossiter as 1970s priest is a didactic mirror of modernity's afterburn, a popular mystery play, in the form of Bakhtin's grotesque realism: embodied instruction to spiritual experience through popular form.

Noise 7

I studied the moulding sheets of the Rossiter monograph... Flip the pages and Akkadian dust flies out... Clogging travel tapes with graveyard sawdust... Southend Detachment on a cassette?... spliced with The Council of Trent bringing up its 9 darter...ancient documents put on computer... Coming to you live from ITV4.

Pulp Reformation

The mystery plays of the 1970s are a "pulp" version of modern Hermeticism, if pulp is both the technological dissemination of the darkly comic vernacular *and* as mode itself of textual production, a material methodology as damp's myth.

The counter-cultural and modernist insertion of occulture into the cultural paradigm has a longer lineage, dating back to a Reformation consciousness. The Protestant Reformation of the sixteenth century accidentally galvanised this mystical enfolding of the quotidian and the weird, as has been outlined through comedy. German theologian Martin Luther's theology cracked down on illegitimate outpourings. Luther's demarcation of secular and spiritual, with the former a space of jurisdiction outside of mysticism. The secular, then, was realm of law-abiding material world, which "God [...] has not sent the holy spirit to interfere with." A spirited, in all senses, engagement with hermeneutics was then reserved within the thresholds of the "*predig ampt*" — the office of preaching.

The arcane lectionary of damp transgresses Luther's "*predig ampt*" with its comic imbrication of the spirit into the material scripted realm, partaking of the technological outpouring that the *pulp* of the printing press offered: a contraption which both gave Luther himself transmission and promulgation, but which he attempted to police thereafter, as part of his draconian mores to delegitimise effete vocalising, spirited speech and magical tropes. The Reformation blackened church ritual with the monochrome of text and strict biblical hermeneutics. Despite the Lutheran revolution of the printing press, Jesuits such as Ignatius of

Loyola[5] outlined a meditation practice of almost psychedelic hallucinatory visions that in their form were anti-textual exercises, visualising intense dramaturgy all the more to focus on the hellfire of eternity. *Rising Damp* as mystery play owes something to this psychic patterning in its showmanship, and of course, in its projection of pictures as opposed to the monochrome of Lutheran text: but it is also in this (damp) text that *Rising Damp* opens up out again to hallucinatory form, finds in base matter's writings the moving pictures of a subjective and formal pulping.

This Counter-Reformation notwithstanding, mysticism is thus distilled into an aberrate form in the late modern period, broadcast itself through the printing press, which deterritorialised the word of God from established sources of authority into the plural dissipation of inscription. Transposed from its medieval hermeneutical context — an embodied and communal activity, focused often within religious women's orders such as the beguine — into an availability of personal transformations, mystical practice as a scrying of the self, or as Bataille calls it "inner experience", is favoured by the increasingly self-focused moderns, to be "masters of this world themselves", evidenced in a Babel of proliferating *Flugschriften* or pamphlets. Officially divorced from its monastic framework, mystical practice, as a personalised experiment and an aesthetic self-knowledge, spurred by the plague of pamphleteers, are paper and ink unfurling, *qua* Civil War Ranter Abezier Coppe's Fiery Flying Roll — the thin de(sur)facements of curling damp scripts, pasted on pub walls, trances and exegesis as an unstoppable stream of mythopoesis

---

5   Ignatius of Loyola is also one of the Saints depicted in Fr. Rolfe's four banners, or stained arras, painted for St Winefride's shrine in Holywell.

pulp(ed) from the mulch of thought as a new epistemological space of the individual. Swapping popish for pulpish, *post-Reformation mysticism is pulp fiction.* Pulp, as a genre of popular fiction, so termed because of the cheap fibrous industrial production of paper, is symbolised in the explosion of cheaply produced high-turnover fiction in the mid-twentieth century, of which Pan Books are cunning exemplar, a Machiavellian import of Damp's code.

ALAN PARTRIDGE: My book is not being destroyed, its being pulped.

This episode of *I'm Alan Partridge*, "Alan Wide Shut" (2002), gives a new meaning to pulp*ed* fiction, where the term as a verb can have resonance in relation to damp.[6] The scandalous incursion of microbial patterns onto walls and door frames corrodes from within, pulping (de(sur)facing) consensual realty and foregrounding the inscriptive nature of time. This creeping stain as a spiritual technology giving access to a mode of life, which does not deny the importance of the industrial popular fiction's output as a genre, but instantiates it as one flare up of damp's code, which, with the cut-up in tow, is running the gamut of avant-garde and popular modernist textual forms and modes. Both pulp and the cut-up are transformative, with the latter contextually dependent

---

6   Steve Coogan's comic character is treated as a "real" person in *Code: Damp*, such is his relevance to the portrayal of crap Englishness aligned uniquely to an understanding of regional TV and comedy, as much as to Coogan's ability to have moved Alan out of the scripted fantasy into an imbrication with "real" media characters across the media Alan appears in.

on the former for its existence as a counter-cultural mode: the transmutation of time into space is de(con)structive.

In opening the floodgates to personal interpretation as technological dissemination, post-Reformation pulp foregrounds this ancient writing surface support that Rigsby's bubbling walls afford and replicate: cheaply fibrous paper for the late age, a divinatory mirror reflecting the future. Pulping as de(sur)facement operates as a form of comedic textual production.

To go further backwards, with the bog's cut-up pulping prosody, Damp's code pre-empts the post-Reformation fragmentation of the mystic. Predicated on the rotting damp text is a Promethean agency armoured with the dis-orienting powers of technology from the putrid mud, which, as reliant and transformative with technics of the self, demarcates an always already flickering of the comedic duality of quotidian and the marvellous, as much as sacred and spiritual, the given and the made.[7]

Such resonance, for a comparison just prior to *Rising Damp*, is Benjamin Britain's trinity of "Church Parables" written between 1964 and 1968. A dramaturgy of cold, damp landscapes, with men dressed as women in the male-only monastic dramaturgy, Britten channelled British sensibility and trilling rebellion into *Curlew River* with this Japanese Noh theatre treatment of a mystery play set in the East Anglian wilds of the Suffolk marshes. A balletic M.R. James seam matching English modernism with fusty tradition, Benjamin insisted it only be performed in churches. He reframed multiple

---

7   The Arthur Machen pastiche "A Yellow Creeper", written in 1895 by Arthur Ricket, describes the "gurgling mysteries [...] that dwell in cheap books".

genres, bringing an avant-garde mysticism to a popular (albeit medieval) instructional dramaturgy, hymning a strange version of the 1960s into the parish, weird evidence that, *pace* Romantic philosopher Schelling, mystery cults are a re-useable grammar, a linguistic *Ur*-form, revealing "a primordial system older than all written documents, which is the common source of all religious doctrines and representations".

As both intoxicated psychopomp and enactor, Rigsby is reusing the grammar of the marsh, a mysticism that is more often used to keep in check the spirit of place, the Green Man Gargoyle as sleeper agent. The sitcom, despite seeming godlessness, retains this mystical perception. Recalling the bivalent vicissitudes of capitalism, such self-knowledge cuts a channel of individuating, whilst atomising the individual in the stream of commercial imperatives. But with the Lutheran reformation onwards, mystical thinking is a synchronic harlequinade that sees the ooze of damp irrigate the soul as individuative process, staining the pulpy everyday with the comedic folk horror of salvation and chip paper. Luther's miserable clamping down is a nihilistic cosmology akin to the episode's killjoy Welsh Evangelical, but the latter accidentally allows the patina of damp to be read against the index of our own souls. *Rising Damp* is more than an epochal metaphor of the epoch's psyche, so much so that by the 1970s, arcane marsh is seeping into life with the pungent staleness of browning mass-market pulp of paperbacks. Filtering dust and glue into bedsit rooms, the hermeneutics of comedy are read in pulp's disorienting fault lines, from dust of Mesopotamia: a damp that smells like Roquefort from the next room.

Now, however, pulp beached on the shores of syncretic cultural appropriations has seen off transmissions from the mythic plane of the marsh, via the churning alchemy of disappointment, into an officially anodyne plane, in the Arcadian sneer and the "National Trust Disco" of period-costume dramas.

Noise 8

The Essex islands get bigger, like torn paper flying, mapping out fragments of Leonard Rossiter's lost mystery play. The paper was in tatters, in ribbons of typewritten script (Reporter writes: these fragments are guidebooks to the territory):

The apostate explains to the Essex Parish why the ceremonial Beach has been prepared:
"The light of Babylon has shone on these endless mudflats. I can see you now have the last dark flame of nostalgia psychosis, so you need cuneiform re-entry to spark time's imagination."
Acolyte adds: "So liquid hymns reiterate Chaldean Acts and get rids of trendy bullies for tomorrow's living."
Apostate adds: "The carrier bags of **Big News** *2 have surfaces whose lineaments reveal a dark fault in the holy countenance. Semi-colon Amen…"*
Apostate adds: "Tell me about them, as I exit the Dionysian locale of the premises?"
"I test drove it with a kebab…"

Realistic evil.

Essex Gnosticism

Going Up

The marsh air rises, and no more so than in Essex. The terrain's *Rising Damp* clothes the endless mud flats in a malefic miasma that manifests a contagious reality. Since the sixteenth century, the noisome and noxious dis-ease of the Essex marsh areas have been variously called "agues", "tertian fevers", "quartan fevers" or "intermittent fevers": John Norden, one of the first cartographers (and thus a key *dis-orienteer* of Essex), commented in 1590 that he couldn't "comende the healthfulness of it: especiallie nere the sea coastes [...] and other loweplaces about the creeks which gave me a most cruell quarterne fever".

The power of the Essex marsh air's "diaphanous folds" of malefic affect is resonantly illustrated by Daniel Defoe in his partly fictional 1722 pilgrimage through vicinal Essex, his *Tour Through the Eastern Counties of England*, which details the "Essex ague" being carried by those who were exposed to this "*damp* part of the world" in marsh villages just north-east of Southend. Like Rigsby, the marsh men, harriers and fowlers, inhabited a circumscribable symbolic zone: traversing the largely reclaimed land of Essex, offset only occasionally when they emerged like goblins from the swamp to mitigate their malaria aches with doses of laudanum.

Pilgrimage is archaeology on the move, evinced in generative de(sur)facements, in as much as the former makes geography mythical, investing its sediments with intent. The stain of time within place, felt underfoot in a disrupted deposit of material, is a feeling of temporal simultaneity. This movement, adequate to the inscription of writing into surface support, or to the trace of sound on the magnetic strip of tape, or the equivalent of TV static and archaeological geophysics, is tapped into through the course, which mutates the spirit of site into a human experience. A form of Englishness, for example, rewinds back as far as medieval Chaucer's outlining of archetypes of spiritual geography in *The Canterbury Tales*, arguably a cousin to the spectator sport of the mystery plays.

Geophysical methods use magnetometers, earth resistance meters and Ground Penetrating Radar systems, in operations that overlap with televisual transmission technology. Resistance of ancient sites as data broadcast as signals is converted into recognisably topographical pictures, an image-making reliant on disruption — on noise. This function suggests something about the landscape as a device for revealing ancient human patterns. Distortion and noise occasion new understandings, according to the level of technics extant at that time, like the clank of the trowel on a buried relic. The terrain becomes a device as much as the sitcom, eschewing the recording as a fatalistic repetition, but as a mutating set of connections and resonances: resonances that are also of the marsh itself, and unknowable by the human. *Rising Damp* gives us to understand our own relation to cultural terrain at that time, and recursively now, in ways unavailable previously to the 1970s. Travel to a sacred landscape, be it to Stonehenge in 4000BC, or to a rave in 1994, or across cyber pages, accrues the patina of time that only the landscape is cognisant of, but which we mutate into uncanny empiricisms.

Joseph Conrad's riverine drive into the *Heart of Darkness*

begins along these Essex shores, rightly apportioning the terrain as the terrifying and transformative route into processes that occur over a vast time and space. Conrad cites the Victorian Essex mist, damply rising and in torrid stasis, "draping the low shores in diaphanous folds": the rising distillation like the churning solve of the alchemical process that are surely a spagyric element to individuation. Part of the alchemical preparation involved collecting the dew of the morning on wet rags. Rigsby's cardigan is heavy with the Essex dew, in sympathetic green. All that remains are the tactics of the hermetic every day. Mutability at work through form, which here is the magic-material matter of the marsh mud and its later indexing in miserable walls: an anabatic modality fogging up individuation.

Essex vicars, precursors to *Father Ted* and the wrong side of Vatican II, fell foul to the vicissitudes of misery and mist over the centuries. According to M.J. Dobson's "History of malaria in England" (1989), by the seventeenth and eighteenth

Anabasis.

century, parish registers in Essex show death in marshland areas to be three times that of dry areas: "from time to time the vicar scribbled in the burial record that the deceased died from 'fatigue' or was just 'worn out'". Rectors of Southend and the locales purportedly refused to take up residence in marshland parishes: "Vicar does not reside in parish because air is too unhealthy," explains one parish register from the time.[1] This clerical titbit denotes a facet of the "Parochial" as both connoting church matters and something beyond this, located in locale, reattached to the mud.

By the nineteenth century, this contagion of the marshes was confirmed as Plasmodium Malaria: "Many observed the characteristic enlargement of the spleen, the anaemic and lethargic condition of the patient [...] The expression 'ague-cake' was often used to describe the prominent spleen of the malaria victim.". This ague come from the from the rising damps of history: linking the noisome effect to the parochial life, engrained as it is in their ludic and empire-circumnavigated tinkering with the hyperbolic odea of the Holy Land. Not forgetting that Mal-aria in the liver and spleen traces back to time's stain, its de(sur)facement — miasma, a Greek term deriving from *miaino*, to stain, insists on the dirty smear, perverse sediment, dissatisfied situation (comedy): the conjunction of gnosis and location, via damp's miasmic modality. Rigby could have both the "ague-cake" of the malarial victim and potentially also liver problems, given

---

1   I dreamt I was defending the marsh's operations whilst walking along a marsh embankment, in the company of a wan Church of England Curate, 6th December 2021.

his propensity for drink.[2] The patina of time gives the infernal method away, but no time is better "wasted" than waiting in the pub, for its pronouncement of the quotidian and the mystical.

A great deal of the Essex marshes, like *Rising Damp*, are at a loss in this post-industrial scene, skirting container ports, barge routes, A-roads. The day before *Rising Damp* first aired, a set of Ranters were recording Essex RnB songs that would feature on their debut album, *Down by the Jetty*. Dr. Feelgood fused pub rock and blues to form a soundtrack for their home, Canvey, a large island in the Thames Estuary drained by the seventeenth-century Dutch, and then gradually inhabited by East End émigrés over the twentieth century. Confidents of Oil City, where Occidental Refinery had been built in 1970, Dr. Feelgood's "Thames Delta" blues dig a different kind of heat — the dis-orientation of this industrial marshland and the desolation of refinery sites, post-demolition.

Where the drab incipient wasteland is hinted in language, or the (meta)physical structure of the sitcom, this effect is directly mercurial and elemental, at the fringes psychologically and physically of the county. A location of boats, flotsam, chemical fires. The undervalued, *inutile*, miserable Essex marshes. Near equivalent for the bleak Id of the dark consciousness M.R. James evokes in Suffolk eeriness, but is, as Spitting Image reminds us, "crap" — more fungible candidate than any other county for the weird strains of the pulped and popular in this "damp part of the world".

In Hermeticism, the theory of correspondences ratifies the marsh as a set of hieroglyphics to be deciphered, making the

<hr>

2   Miasma is also, appropriately, Timothy Morton's second named
     Hyperobject, after Agrilogistics (2016).

endless shiny mud flats a hall of mirrors and, in the words of archaeology magus Tony Robison, "a heck of a place". These bleak flatlands are not just stand-ins for the primal Mesopotamian marshland, nor are they simply haunted Victorian imaginal scenes, but psycho-topographies of the contemporary. A site as myth and method, spatial catalyst for the damp's baseline whose psychic and affective boundaries far transgress the cartographic limits of the county. A baroque boundary that equates gnosis to location.

Rachel Falconer, scrying the twentieth century's fall from grace, traces the pathology of modernity and its symbolic misery through comparison to the ancient Greek mode of katabasis. The latter, a ritual descent, envisages other depths of reality, a pilgrimage to the underworld as specific spiritual locations, which, by virtue of the hermetic descent of the soul, are reached. As Falconer commented, katabasis is not as just a metaphor, but a real access to excess. The Underworld katabasis in Greek myth marks a trip from interior land to coastline. The marsh, this geological fringe between land and sea, is a living regulatory organ for the water inflow and its intensity on the "fractal" coastline.

In liberal humanism's de-sacralisation of life, pulp mysticism is a double-edged sword, but one that is injurious if such location is lost in the slipstream of algorithmic geo-localisable control of subjectivity. Without the leaky plumbing of the soul, as much as the skeleton, "we'd ooze all over the floor", as Rigsby says in "The Prowler". Such Essex Gnosticism counters the ooze of symbolic misery, locating the magic of place across the marsh as a de(sur)facing writing tablet, equivalent to the UR cassette strips, or sitcom TV tapes, whose reeling is a tape pilgrimage to re-edit the marsh's spatio-temporality.

The marsh as this ultimate symbolic and technical zone,

also proffers katabasis's inverse: anabasis — a rising (damp) or a "Going Up", as gnomically intoned in the opening credits to the 1972 BBC sitcom *Are You Being Served?*, punctuated by the clatter of the tills, and the litany of commodities on each floor of the department store. Later models of shop service, *The Fast Show*'s "Suit You Sir" pair are a wilting sensibility, a community of imposition. Behaviour further coloured by the characters' appearance in Holsten Pils adverts through 1999–2001. Holsten then had a veneer of glamour. From 1970s export lager to vogue Brit beer, long before the apotropaic plague of craft beer. Now a libation largely relegated to corner shops, Holsten's lagered generosity maintains through its psychometric presence in photos of Mark E. Smith, in half remembrances of my grandfather enjoying the occasional can, cracking it over the phone to my mother as suburban foley.[3] *Are You Being Served?*'s union here of late industrial commercial patterns, the social structure of high-end shopping, and the British sitcom theme tune as supplicatory rot for the symbolic death toll of these experiences. The scabrous dissipating boundaries of the Essex marsh are also proof that England is decaying, a metaphor for consciousness, which the grimy sets of Colin Piggott superimposed as peeling hallways.

De-composition of rotting damp matter marks the coordinates of this dirty smear of de(sur)facement. Paratextual incursion through damp is a model for the psyche, obliquely affirming the anti-dogma that Freud dismissed as the marshy "black tide of the mud of occultism". Take the fragments of

---

3   Added to which, my grandfather's kitchen walls — gum and cardboard-thickened with cut-out Heinz and Mr Kipling food labels — were de(sur)faced with hand written warning signs. "Don't eat cheese late at night, it gives you *nightmares*."

paper I have fished out of the marshy bracken on the fringes of Essex. Parts of Leonard Rossiter's lost mystery play, or remnants of an ancient saga, the papers pulpcd in damp storms, gradually accruing brine and bacteria. Damp on these fantastical documents is corroding the difference of timelines. The scraps of paper washed up on the estuary shoreline could be Eric Chappell's original sitcom scripts, a vade mecum of displaced modernism. In the psycho-topography of damp, the dissolving scraps of paper are a visual analogue to its corrosive metaphysics. Total capture is evaded when such mediations of standard format eschew clear distinctions between beginning and end, author and world.

Noise 9

His empty eyes are tuned to more television channels than exist in your world. Right here among you... A TV channel for riverine Essex: wort prevision, tidal surveyor... Aye!

Sitcom Mystics

When asked where the *Rising Damp* was set, creator and screenwriter (and former electricity employee) Eric Chappell, said: "nowhere" (although he implied it could be near Leeds, where the sitcom was filmed). Such "nowhere" is apt for the Essex wasteland as regional metaphor, but more, as a location of spiritual gnosis. To Rigsby's hieroglyphics, oozing up through the walls, a domestic flare-up of this drab English mysticism is evident in Essex, a record in and of cut-up landscape. The mud carrying the germ of cuneiform's curse, but such spurious externalising of memory onto surfaces has its counterpoint in mystical forgetting. *The Cloud of Unknowing*, a fourteenth-century English text of mysticism, said to be written by a monk or rector "somewhere" in Northern England, insists upon this fundamental duality of unknowing and forgetting: "*When you are nowhere physically, you are everywhere spiritually.*"

Speaking of which, something is lying snagged on a marsh reed. Like the alchemical cloth for collecting dew, like Rigsby's cardigan, like Fr. Rolfe's stained arras, a black carrier bag from Southend's *Big News 2* off-licence, is soaking up the miasmic atmosphere. Air heavy with the Essex ague condensates and de(sur)faces. Across the black polyethylene is relief-printed in crude replica the eponymous "Cloud", black-letter as *Rising Damp*, from *The Cloud of Unknowing*: specifically, a copy of the 1960s Penguin Classics edition, a mass-market paperback with black and purple cover, and brown, pock-marked pages. The lino-printed legend, from the eponymous pulp binding of Medieval words, meets much-needed alcoholic dissolution: what a relief! Something of *Code: Damp*'s agon is embodied in this febrile publication, magical stand in for the mystery play scripts of the 1970s, re-surfaced on a grotty carrier bag. The most available yet paratextual mode to carry your Pan Horror book, cuneiform tablet and can of Holsten, such that the carrier bag willingly merges all examined figures thus far into bathetic *gestalt*. The mundane and the mystical flare up on the plastic surface, to collide layered registers of mysticism's mid-century pulp. The purple ink's cracks are like geological fault lines in small scale, psychic and socio-existential cracks that lead through to these mythic depths of Essex.

Rising Damp de(sur)faces carrier bag: a breakdown in reception that the Cloud of Unknowing is prophetic vapour to.

Take the waters – have the *Odd Lager*, Rigsby certainly does, but this isn't surprising as the Akkadian edict is already written on his walls. Rigsby, as much as Mark E. Smith, are later instantiations of *The Cloud of Unknowing*'s mystical Northern scribe: like Old Testament "types", or mystical precursors of older and future mythic characters. A spatiotemporal vector that tunnels through the brown palette of the walls and curtains, back to the squalid vegetation of the mire, synchronising disparate space-times as much as any good post-modern hybridisation. Out of the marsh bricolage comes miasmic interfusions for the mystic's journey to the heart of darkness. Rigsby draws out this constant and laudable reintegration of mystical tropes into the condensation of the blearily domestic modern sitcom — a lineage that has long been a tinkering with the formation of the self as channel of the code. Part of an ongoing UR Mix Tape, a damp diversion cognisant of mescaline-coloured author Aldous Huxley's formulation of the universal affinity of all spiritual systems. His 1945 *The Perennial Philosophy* suggested a long line of adepts of "perennial philosophers" in the likes of Julian of Norwich, William Blake, Philip K. Dick, who all espouse a trans-temporal and spatial mysticism.

If this is the mystic's prop, the attendant ritual behaviours for *Rising Damp* as modernity's mystery play deploy everything from divination and seances to boxing matches and fasting, abetted by psychotropic effects of damp, drink and drugs. But if calls for a revivification of metastable potentials in counterculture draw on acid and psilocybin, as much as to a fulsome excitement of potential pre-globalisation, the spagyric churning of life untimely as irreverent and disturbing oscillates around Machen's dialectic of humour and the hermetic. The microbial phylum instantiates a fear of dissolution, but what seems like a formless non-life, is deformation at the level of Art Brut: symbols being undone and redone, a mannerist dissolution, reached as a cellular consciousness, in particular with mushrooms, with Machen, and even Tony Hancock — mushrooms and lichen are a key enlisting of the marsh, the undead growth and the comic. Hancock is reminded of the poor state of his house, when Bill Kerr counsels him not to forget the "mushrooms growing on the walls" — to which he replies, "Yes, it's like Hackney marshes in there, some nights!" (BBC, 1957).

> *RUTH: It's so dark damp and dark down there — even the mushrooms don't look very good this year.*

Melting walls and breathing curtains aren't just the limit experience of mind-altering substances, but the sensation of the damp's domestic mysticism. A model for comic existence, which can be verging on the unhuman. The hallucinogenic affect seeps out of the walls of the sitcom: time's stain getting you high, causing psychotropic visions — *The Daily Mirror* cautions in 2019: "Black mould in your home can cause terrifying hallucinations of demons and ghosts". Such second sight comes from huffing misery's vapours, as much as it is proof of Rigsby's active imagination.

> *RIGSBY: (to Alan) Sometimes I don't think you exist; I think you come out of the bloody wallpaper.*

For Rigsby, being Jung at heart, such an affordance allows us to glimpse a joyous if not untroubled metaphysics immanent to the decomposing and diseased lineaments of the TV set. In his role as psychopomp, Rigsby burns the sacrificial perfume of the "love wood" in the hope of seducing Miss Jones, only to find he's been conned by Philip into incensing a planed strip of wardrobe. The perfume is a sacrificial offering to the Money God of personal failure. 1970s tat shouldn't be too hastily inhaled. The psychedelic fumes dilate time, whilst Rossiter, in an anecdote recalled by scriptwriter Eric

Chappell, famously talked at double the speed of anyone else, as if on some high-quality amphetamine, meaning that the programme recording came in too quick to fit in with the commercial breaks. As if he were in a different psychotropic signature to the rest of the cast.

> RIGSBY: (to Alan) You'd have too much LSD and try walking through a wall.

As much as the iris dilates under the influence, Rigsby's models, in past and future, pierce open holes in the temporal fabric of the everyday: Jacobean Abbess Susanne Katherina von Klettenberg calls mystical practices detached from normative religious frameworks — *viz* post-Reformation pulp — a mode of experiential epistemology, an art of living. Lucian, in Arthur Machen's tale, turns to masochism and starvation to induce mystical ecstasies, as does Rigsby, when he tries to win a bet of £5 that he can go for twenty-four hours without food. Moss even crawls over Rigsby's fine line in green cardigans, if not hair shirt. Even his water turns green when he's secretly given tranquillisers when seducing Miss Jones: the only instance of actual drug taking. His reactions are slowed to a deadened pulmonary frequency, and he is unable to ascertain that the Matt Monro record he's been duped into playing is on at the wrong speed, before eventually keeling over onto Miss Jones's lap.[4]

---

4   This hallucinatory timestamp could just as likely inversely invoke the work of David Munrow — stalwart medieval revivalist, and radio "Pied Piper" who sadly killed himself in 1976, but not before piping anachronism into the 1970s through his early music revivalism. Of particular note is Granada TV series *Early Musical Instruments*, filmed

A soothing spectacle channelling our collective and
forgivable folly, stricken with the shamanic knowledge of
the Fall: Rigsby's brain pulses mouthed platitudes with no
sound coming out. Drink and drugs, are abetted by modern
divination. "Suddenly at Home" sees a hypochondriac lodger,
Osborne, seemingly cop it, after Rigsby has repeatedly jibed
him about his multiple hospital visits.

*RIGSBY: They probably already got someone down for your kidneys
and your liver....And there won't be any questions — like what's
happened to your liver.*

Whilst endlessly referring to Osborne's liver, he cites the
fantastical number of X-rays Osborne has had.

*RIGSBY: What he's paid in wouldn't cover the X-rays! He must
have every part of his anatomy X-rayed by now. They cover a
whole wall down at the hospital — it's like a full-scale map of the
underground.[5]*

A rote psychogeographic trope, the reproduction of internal

---

at Ordsall Hall, Salford in 1976. In front of beige, Tudorbethan, and
trefoil wooden backdrops lit by candlelight, Munrow obsessively charts,
describes and plays a wide number of woodwind instruments, and
keyboards, inter alia, with his instrumentalists lined up in brown suits.
A unique invocation, it rests somewhere in the interstices of lecture,
concert, rant and breakdown.

5   Cockney artist and magician Austin Osman Spare (1886-1965) was
affectionately sent up in Oswell Blakestone's "Magicians in London"
(1950) for his domestic mysticism: "Come back one day," he invited,
"and I'll show you all your future in a vision on the wall. You'd like that
wouldn't you? All your future spread out like a map before you..."

Bog Body.

organs as a microcosm for projecting into time and its spatial coordinates are a route out of symbolic misery, a fortune-telling, but not out of necessary duration. "One man can change the world with a bullet in the right place," says Mick Travis in Lyndsey Anderson's *If* (1968).[6] Like a miniature bullet path, or the incision of the cut-up, dictating the sightline through strata of time, these transformative holes are also pierced through sheep's livers in ancient Mesopotamian fortune-telling. Hepatoscopy — from the Greek for liver: *hêpar* — was a divination technique practiced as early as the third millennium BC in Babylonia. One cuneiform tablet which indexes this practice — the infamous clay "Liver Tablet", an eighteenth-century-BC fortune-teller's instruction tool — was

---

6   *Performance* (1970) by Donald Cammell, who was influenced by the
     writing of Antonin Artaud, is an occult-crime counterculture film
     starring James Fox and Mick Jagger, and uses the same motif of a bullet
     hole as the portal to a transformative reality.

used to read the future through the certain holey "zones" represented on the tablet as separate boxed areas that contain cuneiform letters to indicate what "protrusions, patches of colour, pustules and scars" would foretell. Such vision entailed a "second sight", a *tele*-vision, as a clairvoyance of the miraculate beyond the Flat Time of the everyday.

The liver, here and in *Rising Damp*, as a clay road map for individuation, grounds *sacrifice* into the marsh: its bog standard propaganda that primordial man take part in the "Accursed Share", the necessary tipping-over into excess expenditure, but also in the mud that is the moment of spiritual schism, or *tele*-vision.

To bely the distinction between the given and the made — to suggest that the marsh was always a mystical *tele* — we have a perverse atavistic alienation born against any existential authenticity. A division that begets alienation, deracination. The Greek God Prometheus as the augur of technics, the bringer of fire, has his liver eaten away every day as punishment, yet it constantly renews. This liver is termed by Bernard Stiegler an "organic mirror". A surface of divinatory hermeneutics matched by the wider slippery surface of the marsh, a de(sur)facement reflecting time across shiny mudflats. A marsh tape strip, or a huge page of sitcom script, formed by channels of water that cut into its body, carve its skin — like the incisions of ancient script, snaking through the mud.

P.V. Glob's *The Bog People* in 1965, now a lauded study, contains Glob's suggestion that most "sacrificed humans" were put to death to satisfy the "Earth Mother" — the goddess shown on the Gundestrup cauldron, unearthed in a bog not far from the burials of various of these sacrificed individuals, thus preserved because the carbohydrate polymer sphagnum from the moss of the same name, which binds nitrogen, halts the growth of bacteria, and mummifies the corpse in a kind of marsh-stasis. *Contra* this stasis, the mud can also be a bacterial buzzing of decay, metabolising churning rot as much as any New Materialist conceptions of sentient slop, despite itself.

Rigsby as Hepatoscopist, abetted by the psychotropic obliterations of the self, with candles flickering in the basement. Sundry offal placed on the table, illuminated by a grimy LWT programme, maps out a psychic landscape of damp from mystical modernity. Research on later human Iron Age marsh sacrifice came to fruition along with the counter-culture.[7] With such sacrifice, being subject to delay, but eschewing reality-blocking conditioning of digital entertainment, you can go back to an anterior state of the body, but, it's a double-edged sword in the sacrificial bog: "If you live by the Bog Axe, you die by the Bog Axe," as Alan Partridge told Tony Robinson in an episode of *Mid Morning Matters*.

Leaking holes and scars opening up the subject to delay, the trace of inscribed time laid out simultaneously, in reflecting graffitied time as differentiation: like perfume let lose in the air whose eddies slowly unfurl (*per fumum*) through the (sacrificial) smoke — a condensation becomes apparent, the blind spot of personal failure, like the aporia that founds the origin of the human. The holes of this prophetic giveaway are also nodes for expression, humour and despair. Feeling, for the classicists, is located in the organ of the liver, the seat of the feeling of situation, which secretes black bile, *melas kholie*. We create the sublime by sublimating gratification, as laid out above, in Flattening Time: deferring desire, the lack, potent in the sediment, is a rich fault line to channel against sad contemporary passions. A slow drop effect which will

---

7   The Iron Age is circumspectly between 1200 and 600 BC.

itself have an indexical mark upon the liver, in time. Rigsby's ague cake as the marsh inhabitant makes him a Bog Body, insufflated with miasmic *Essex* ague.

Faust and Loose

His Essex Gnosticism is unorthodox because it insists on the contaminating power of material as also implicit in the psychic world, as a direct assault on aspiration in a bourgeois and spiritual sense by a tuning into time's matter flow. His love of drink, his communion with his lodgers, opens up to a faculty of feeling itself, and how these mystical percepts in the everyday can alter and create a whole aesthetic response to reality. Joyous carousing seeks mysticism through self-sacrifice at the level of duration.

The "nowhere" of the marsh, and modernity's mystical tactics, are indurate to all but this engrained duration. The spiritual technology of damp and its "diaphanous folds" momentarily sway in the drab tenement curtains. *Rising Damp* is like a brightly coloured stained-glass window, offering transtemporal access to this, popular culture's esotericism. Marsh cuneiform writing is the "real" of writing, coming from this hypnagogic zone, four millennia hence, rising up in damp to be televised across supports and surfaces for writing, as much as the contemporary digital world sinks down to the Akkadian depths through heathen rubble.

End of Part One

The Indoor League.

ADVERT BREAK
Seynt Lyonard's Hagiography

Rubber Band

For this mystical appreciation, a new addition to Huxley's Perennial "Natural Theology of the Saints", Rossiter is transubstantiated though the eucharist of the advert. Rigsby and Reggie's guiding spirit is revealed as the electrical current, the fount of energy, to light up the mythic plane of the sitcom.

Leonard begins his "career" (if such a pedestrian term can be applied to magick, and perhaps it can, if the mundane nourishes the more-than-real) in an amateur group, the Centre Players, followed by Preston Repertory Company and Wolverhampton Repertory Company, the Salisbury Repertory Company and then Bristol Old Vic Company. In a few years, he toured British theatres in a crucifying schedule of script-learning and performing. His first nineteen months in the business saw Len play over seventy-five roles, appearing in the Playhouse Salisbury; Alexandra Theatre, Birmingham; Bristol Old Vic; Theatre Royal, Bristol; Leatherhead Theatre Club; the Playhouse, Nottingham; and the Belgrade Theatre, Coventry. A pattern commensurate to the mystery plays that temporarily inhabited regional towns: further hauntologically layered by Leonard's transferal to small screen in the early 1960s, in a huge popularity of TV plays, during which time he proved his worth as a so-called "straight" actor.

He joined rep whilst still working as a claim inspector in a Liverpool insurance firm, translating in acting a dutiful ardour, the grammar of the British office: "he brought eccentricity to the role — the sort of expression you find in ordinary people". In Ibsen's *Ghosts*, he prepared perfect insurance documents as props for Pastor Manders. Leaning on props that are rotten as preparation, surely, as for the pen-pushing logistics of Reggie Perrin's office job at Sunshine Desserts. Metonymy of his office days recurs again and again in his language, and in others' descriptions: his taught body movements are referred to as "rubber band-like"; he has the "elastic features of a British silent film caricaturist"; and he described the operation of learning a litany of theatre scripts in Rep as like "Sellotape" — "We just stuck them on and then tore them off. It was the perfect preparation for rehearsing situation comedy on television at the rate of an episode a week," he told *The Sunday Telegraph*.

> *DENHOLM ELLIOTT: I've always been very careful in my career to do theatre; it takes you out of the television eye.*

Rossiter's Liverpudlian roots, and their filtering through black-and-white fantasy of kitchen-sink Albion *Billy Liar* before alighting on the bubblegum colours of Stanley Kubrick's *Barry Lyndon* and *2001: A Space Odyssey* via Lyndsey Anderson, draws together planes of mid-twentieth-century filmmaking, British Edition. The weather in Rossiter's soul rises to the surface, lightning affords vision distinct to the unregulated geo-localisable markets of the post-industrial. An animism through videotape brought to life in Anderson's *O Lucky Man!*, a scabrous path, an ersatz factory pilgrimage of Britain. This was mirrored in the film that would feature Leonard as hospital PR manager Vincent Potter in the trilogy's part three, 1982 satire on the cynical expediency of government: *Britannia Hospital*. The nightmare journeying in *Lucky Man*, in the unregulated world of a borderless global economy, of coffee salesman Mick Travis (Malcolm McDowell) — *A straunge sighted traueller* — meeting reiterative, chaotic, almost occulted British decay, is a dark mirror to industrial pandemonium and the regional and professional oddness that was Leonard's own training ground.

Muddy Companion

Leonard Rossiter prioritised the material world, producing a finely tuned physical comedy to tether the flashes of the effervescent mind. Rossiter's body is mettle to the very idea of performance: brittle yet mercurial gestures as tuning fork for supernatural forces, which in turn spurred a highly tense energy; an energy Leonard worked off, like a coiled spring.

His acting could "best be described as volcanic: it alternates between menacing brooding inertia and eruptions of hysterical violence", Frank Marcus, *Sunday Telegraph*, 1969; he is "quite electrifying", says Harold Hobson in *The Sunday Times*; "he gives an example of his electrified comedy", Peter Rodford, *Western Daily Press*, 1960. As sudden and awesome yet inexplicable as lighting. This is not a hammy ode to treading the boards, but the transformation of the meagre everyday into the humorous and the horrific; a forte for the admixture of the comic and the manic. "You could say I'm at my best at strong characters with a manic streak: I like roles such as Hitler where you can go from outraged hysteria to assumed calm in second," said Rossiter in *TV Times*, 1969.

The "comic macabre" of his *Arturo Ui*, in Brecht's parody of Hitlerian mania and the dark brittleness of power, means that Rossiter, like his character Rigsby in *Rising Damp*, "never lets us forget the gas chambers, the bombs, the slaughter" (Clive Barnes, *New York Times*, 1969). This is borne out in many of his generations: Rossiter was a sergeant in the Intelligence Corps, like other comics forged in the furnace of World War II, *pace* Kenneth Williams and Tommy Cooper. With his voice choking back a tidal wave of emotion, and his mouth like a looming shark's grin on mania's crest, the comic is conveyed, *à la* Rigsby, with both brutality and comic impotence in one, abetted by a punctilious and perfectionism in rehearsal and performance, which made Rossiter a sometimes-unbearable colleague. Written with affirmative economy, mirroring his tight delivery, he recommends Keith Floyd's 1981 *Floyd's Food* saying "this book is bound to be good" in his modest foreword for the ebullient chef: a fellow partner in wine.

Michael Blakemore, director of *Arturo Ui*, highlighted Rossiter's parochial training in repertory and the office as galvanising stratigraphy for his later mannerisms: "as an actor he had much in common with the great performance of an earlier generation, a self-sufficient talent forged out of the necessity in the provinces". Sensible also to Rossiter's insurance days, this weird affect is relayed through a Morse code of expulsions, stiff gaits, head nods, twitches and grins inseparate from his travel itinerary. In Arthur Machen's *Hieroglyphics*, the occult writer explains that art is the product of an *invisible companion*, whose feet makes tracks in the "Other World". But in what he terms Pantagruelism, *pace* François Rabelais and Béroalde de Verville, this is transposed into a "*muddy* companion" — a "being often of exquisite wit and deep understanding, but given to evil ways if one does not hold him in check". Arthur Machen's "harlequinade of humanity" betrays a Gnostic Dualism between the composed and the irate, that underlines sitcom's incursion into the mystical mud of the marsh as substratum for humour's different effects.

"He played Grotesques."

The grotesque is the post-classical post-modern facility of collage. From the term for grotto, it outlines the fanciful and terrifying forms found in Roman bath houses, melding faces, ornamentation, foliage and sprites. It is something *out of place*, unnatural, mannered.

"And he kept the tension throughout each performance." Every twitch and curl of the body was choreographed, a microcosm of intent, flooded with electric forces in and out of the television. In most scenes, his body was, as *Rising Damp* scriptwriter Eric Chappell adds, "bent like a question mark".

Mannerisms were noted in Rossiter's performance as Giordano Bruno in *The Heretic*, at the Duke of York's Theatre, 1970. A performance that was all effects and little else. Bruno was burned to death by the inquisition for suggesting the existence of other worlds in the universe. No less glimmering with an epochal brilliance, Rossiter is more parochial, concerned more with duality of the muddy. The heavy heresy of the play is smoothed over by his grimaces, convulsions and satire. Rossiter's St Vitus dance of gaping Hallowe'en leers, machine-gun delivery, facial contortions and enviable ability to walk effortlessly into a room with his body arched back an angle of 45° is the appearance of essence, the glamour of the surface, the marsh and its muddy companion.

Has there been such a grotesquery since the hunchbacked Loughton swung from the gargoyles of Notre Dame?
Felix Barker, *Evening News*, 1969, on Rossiter's *Arturo Ui*.

A Subtle Blend

An intensity not of an open fire but of a concentrated burning glass: an appropriate method in outlining the chimerical breakdown of character, performance and man.

Although his character is a gauche compendium of the mannerism and affectations evident throughout Rigsby and Reggie, Leonard was (always) playing that infra-thin version of himself in these Cinzano adverts, in which he stars with Joan Collins. Transmitted from 1978–1983, they were drawing on and crystallising in commercial form, a popular approval shored up through the years of *Rising Damp* and *The Fall and Rise of Reginald Perrin*. In each thirty-second advert, Rossiter, in a weary "nowhere" of the ingratiating expat, sips Cinzano after having cast a spell of slapstick with the sickly sweet cordial. The meeting of the carnival and the TV, contingency of arm movement and speed, in a gag he stole from the music hall, as much as an inversion of Eddie's advice to Richie in Series 2 of *Bottom*: "Always keep your mouth open when insulting a lady."[1]

---

1   The open mouth is a motif worth bearing in mind for Part 2 of this book, as is the holding structure of the advert itself. The Cinzano advert in question is one demonstrable instance of the cost we pay in commercial life as much as death. But the advert promises some dilation, or suspension, of mortality. An endlessly reputable segment of ersatz inebriation. Costs are writ large on the advertising boards for "Grot", Reginald Perrin's business from Series 2 of the sitcom.

The Cinzano advert demands metanoia for some, a transubstantiation of the past into the present, payment to calm the waters of death. *Lonely Water*, a 1973 children's public information film voiced by 1970s actor Donald Pleasance, limns the terrors of outer-London marsh pools, ready to trap the unwary. Under the water there are traps: bedstead, weed, cars, hidden depths.[2]

"I remember going round to Leonard's house," film director Alan Parker recalls, "and we agreed the scripts were absolute rubbish. So, Leonard said 'What I'd like to do is the old music hall joke', and we said 'What's that?', so he picked up his cup of tea as we were sitting there in his living room, and he looked at his watch, turning the cup over. And we said 'Yeah, that'll be a good joke, especially if it happens to be Joan Collins, you're spilling it on!"

With Cinzano, the open mouth of Joan Collins as the clear liquid flies at her face foretells or conjoins with Reggie's scream, which will be the key note of *The Fall and Rise of Reginald Perrin*. As a sitcom augur of the terrors of mass consumerism, Rossiter is then an odd choice for a commercial — or is he? Other august characters have appeared in commercial beer adverts, such as Donald Pleasance, again, advertising another lonely water — Holsten Pils, in 1980. Still with "The Odd Lager" catchphrase, Pleasance is cut in half in a cheap magician's stage box (before the unfortunate descent into Brit Pop which heralded Ray Winston's "It's the Daddy" Holsten advert).

---

2   The marsh is the River Styx, transit for the Water Man, or even used-car salesman, *Minder*'s Dennis Waterman, narrator to another PIF, *Excuse Me, But That's My Car* (1987).

The walls of marble blacke that moistened still shall weepe.

Rossiter questions, through body and soul, the tenets of consensual reality, crossing over the border between personality and comic character creation. Harnessing the energy of his characters to the thanatological coordinates of modern advertising, he demonstrates the metaphysical world within the TV set, a surrealist-capitalist end-of-the-pier mania: a tension of matter and idea that is the domain of the Muddy Companion.

Traversing the vast mythographic landscape of the advert takes more than a simple guide; only this master psychopomp can negotiate such a passing. Leonard Rossiter is before and after the post-industrial man, that period of the 1970s when versions of counter-culture transformed into the hyper-industrial decadence. Leonard's rapid speech come as "fragments out of time" of time, and corroborates this truth: that the sacred, like the Cinzano artefact, flickers in and out of transmission. Sublimated religion in the modern age of the twentieth and twenty-first centuries is brought to life when the Muddy Companion crawls alongside his host. Here is fleeting proof of the sheer exhilaration of existence, twinned with Britain's torrid parochialism as bathetic counterpoint. Commerce transforms to miracle in a hagiography of *Seynt Lyonard*, providing enough supernatural energy to power whole universes.

PART 2
The Fall and Rise of Reginald Perrin

Noise 1

Bog Bodies demand redress on Southend High Street, from rest, from rest....

Gaiety Bazaar has closed down, sherds of illuminous price tags litter the seaside promenade. One lost purchase, still readable: Willy Warmer £1.99.

Suburban Machiavelli

Ersatz Nowhere

Ancient texts inscribed in muddy depths are eroded by Essex tides; crop circles of the sacred scar many a post-industrial wasteland. This bogside graffiti flashes visions on every television screen in the world.[1] The Akkadian heartlands of mud, inscribed with cuneiform marks, start to feel more credulous than the wavering mists and shipping channels of the contemporary scene.

The river, as the slipstream of England's age-old shipping precinct, ekes out into Conrad's convict territory. Bleak shores where miasmic air hangs in diaphanous folds. The stain of time is a grey smear blurring land, sea and sky. Go upstream west, and you enter the East London Dockland regeneration.

The filter between the City of London and its effulgent riverine stretches, its Thatcherite whitewashing of Victorian

---

1   *Essex, Essex, Essex is crap. It's an absolute abomination. Essex, Essex fall off the map! It's the boil on the bum of the nation* (*Spitting Image*). The glimmering laughter hidden in the grot, the fire lying hidden flints, the writing lying hidden in the marsh: what is actually more crap is the moribund heritage industry of *Spitting Image*'s earlier verses "Kent is renowned as the Garden of England/In Cornwall there's a lot to be seen/Sussex has wonderful coastal resorts/And Devon has beautiful cream/Lancashire has its famous sausages/Yorkshire, the best beer on tap/But the county of Essex is different: Essex is just *crap*."

wharfs and rusting barge jetties into melancholy flat complexes.[2]

This shifting mud of the Docklands, as pinstriped East End gangster Harold Sand (Bob Hoskins) says in *The Long Good Friday* (1979) reflects the neoliberal changes of British capitalism: "We're in the common market now!" he gurns at American investors, with whom he'd hoped to develop part of the Docklands, in a prescient foretelling of 1981's London Docklands Development Corporation quango. The deal falls through, due to the IRA moving in on his patch. A little down the road, the horrific wooden "Dagenham idol" sticking out of the mud in 1922, before the Ford Motor works were built, foretells the dark comedy of Dagenham's other idols, Dudley Moore and Peter Cook's Derek and Clive. This low-lying damp energy-field of history is a constantly transformative elemental that transubstantiates past into present, and re-writes memory, even in absentia. The BBC's tape-wiping of the duo's early work is an embedment of erasure's numinous power. If the marsh is sitcom, it is a bleakly capitalist-surrealist vista, the wider British entertainment history, whether foul-mouthed or gangster glamour, is the dissipating substratum: a hinge zone which, opening up consensual reality, reveals the tectonic shifts of globalisation.

The ice-cream van that is used to remove the corpse of one of Harold's delivery men is presaged by the ice-cream van which Leonard Rossiter's sitcom character in *The Fall and Rise of Reginald Perrin* (1976–1979, BBC) drives to the Devon coast to

---

2   Heavy production and global commerce have now shifted ever further
     out of City sight to make way for heritage housing, such that London
     Gateway, which opened in 2013, is a fully integrated logistics facility
     visible through the mists of Canvey Island.

perform his faked suicide. The van, belonging to his company Sunshine Desserts, of which he is senior sales executive, is a gaiety drive from the weird monotony of commercial production: far away from his gangster contemporaries, but yet a relentless homogeneity of industry, and the stale repetition of life Reggie is screaming to get out of.

A mercurial meeting of coincidences then, when Leonard Rossiter does the voiceover, as city worker Reggie Perrin, for the London Docklands Development Corporation advert in 1982. Fittingly ugly birds that resemble Rod Hull's Emu sit on Nelson's column, riffing on Reggie's repeated commuter catchphrase "*Eleven minutes late…*": catchphrases of both Reggie and C.J., which would have been the common currency of pubs, offices and homes.

> *REGGIE: That New Town me and my friends have moved to, 50 miles as the crow flies. And believe me, I flew it.*
> *VOICEOVER: All business development areas have got one thing in common: they are all not in London. All except the London Docklands.*
> *C.J.: "I didn't get where I am today" by being somewhere else.*
> *VOICEOVER: The London Docklands Development Corporation: why move to the middle of nowhere, when you can move to the middle of London?*

Selling the prospect of living near London, as opposed to the suburbs, the strange commuter-belt satisfaction of C.J. metes out neoliberal agenda through terse sitcom catchphrases, they bely their own roots in suburbia – and in their own commercial failure – for cheap payment.

In the thin, yellow light of the Docklands advert is coded a dreary transit from Essex to a remade London. A commute far more modern than that conducted by Reggie every day in the 1976 sitcom. Scriptwriter Eric Chappell had insisted that *Rising Damp* was set "nowhere", and Reggie's Clinthorpe cul-de-sac echoes a stranger beat than is possible in the globalised city. *When you are nowhere physically, you are everywhere spiritually*, as the rotting ennui of suburbia proves.[3]

The commuter line in *Reginald Perrin* is a fall out from and response to the encroaching homogenisation of the mock-Tudor Home Counties. Unlike the trainline commute of Basildon through to the Dockland's regeneration (past many rubbish dumps, atavistic and future-oriented, black carrier bags poking out of mud), Reggie Perrin's commute is a psychic trip, a katabasis or deathly pilgrimage, between the poles of suburbia and office. His regular beat each morning, down Coleridge Close, right into Tennyson Avenue and right into Wordsworth Drive, en route to the station, brackets his increasingly anagogic gestures: odd behaviours heightened through repetition. Similarities might still accrue, though,

---

3   Essex has attenuated the radical power of strangeness and bleakness far less than the numbing suburban. The homogeneity of culture is distilled, damp and stagnant. The county as an unwitting political barometer for the terminally unimaginative to mock. Many housing estates also appear beached against Essex marshland. Drab brownfield sites built on by successive Tory and Labour governments appear on the horizon, still just within blasting distance of the fog horns, shopping malls at the side of the Thames at Dracula's Purfleet. New Town Basildon, but one of many on the heels of globalisation. On the commuter line from Shoeburyness to Fenchurch Street, it's now a windswept Brutalist precinct with a few charity shops, a Wetherspoons, a pound shop (further north, an industrial estate, and once site of *The Echo*'s premises, where I once got offered a reporting job).

as both estuary Essex and metaphysical suburbia are places that make you re-act, as we are told by the frequent and odd surtitles that change in the opening credits of each *Reginald Perrin* episode, as the mournfully jolly theme tune by Ronnie Hazlehurst plays, setting the beat for a sitcom colliding death and flabby office life with singular levity.

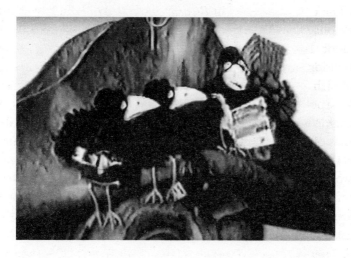

Sacramental disappointments: Docklands Development Corporation advert.

The opening credits, then: Reggie, a jerky, sped-up silent movie figure, runs along a beach, having left the ice-cream van in the car park area, and, discarding his clothes on the shoreline, disappears into the sea. *THE FALL* goes down the screen over the shot of Reggie submersing himself in the freezing English Channel. *AND RISE* tails up the screen as his bobbing form slips away into the distance. Doyen of the mid-life crisis, the anabasis of *Rising Damp* charting a course to plug into the majesty of life, muck and glamour withal.

Reggie Perrin. 46, senior sales executive. Bored. Under stress.

The first TV series is this strange crescendo leading to his faked suicide, leaving his clothes on a beach: an event already witnessed, repeated from the credits of the first episode onwards. A sartorial dissolution known as a "rapture bomb", but is now known proverbially as "doing a Reggie Perrin". "*It's [literally] a dress rehearsal for the last day of judgement,*" as J.G. Ballard wrote in *The Drowned World*. The graveyard humour of faked suicide, always glossed over in the series, keeps in check the grotesquery that was Rossiter's forte, as much as the character's. In Antonin Artaud's terms, this might be passing from the imitation of life into life itself. His desultory clothes like the haunted flapping bedsheets moving on the beach, in the M.R. James story "Oh, Whistle, and I'll Come To You, My Lad" are domestic drapes insufflated by a magician's force, a self-directed expressive force against himself and the world. These are signified in burial wraps, symbols of the surface of normal time being activated, or the leftover costume for an experiment.

REGGIE: I'm fed up of doing things the same way.

Investigating the torrid underbelly of the suburban, lampooned in the Docklands' commercial, is where an enquiry attuned to Reggie's psychic de(sur)facing begins, and ends — where a great deal of disintegration is manifest. This puncturing of reality equates to simple perversions. Reggie constantly fantasising in surreal tableaux, gorging on ravioli, lying to his boss about dinner, and launching into a weirdly paced diatribe against wanton post-modern consumption whilst drunk at a work conference — all essential evidence that transhistorical events felt in the industrial period are most crucial in the everyday, the "parochial". In a vacuum of stale repetition, Reggie ramps up tension by both presupposing and narrating an imminent disaster.

Finding ever more fatuous ways to market poor-quality products, the "exotic ices" campaign that Reggie is tasked with by stentorian company boss C.J. exemplifies the ersatz life of the Clinthorpe cul-de-sac, as well as the life of suburban disappointment of George Bowling in Orwell's *Coming Up for Air* (1939):

GEORGE BOWLING: "I remembered a bit I'd read in the paper somewhere about these food-factories in Germany where everything's made out of something else. Ersatz, they call it. I remembered reading that they were making sausages out of fish, and fish, no doubt, out of something different. It gave me the feeling that I'd bitten into the modern world and discovered what it was really made of."

This gaudy realisation primes one for ersatz living, or makes one forge routes out of it. In J.G. Ballard's story "The Enormous Space", adapted for TV by BBC 4 as *Home* in 2001, the quiet, suburban semi-detached is sensible to landscapes lying behind those of countercultural individualistic affectation. Like Perrin, Gerald Ballantyne of Ballard's story has a comestible-oriented job. Gerald is Principal Product Developing Technologist at Initial Foods. In *Home*, Gerald is seen leaving the door of his house in Surbiton in suit and with briefcase, *qua* Reggie, who does the same in landscape's cardinal opposite, Norbiton. Gerald's retreat into the semi-detached leaves him resolved never to leave it again, to conduct an experiment "in Suburban living", as he describes in the first of a series of digital diary videos. Talking down to the camera from his kitchen breakfast bar, he says: "*It suddenly occurred to me that the entire course of my life could be changed by a single action — using the simplest of weapons, my front door, I could shut out the world and solve all my problems.*"

This conviction is an example of what Henri Lefebvre would call a "mood": a miasma of creativity from which a "situation" might arise. With modernity, revolution ironically becomes an increasingly hazy and distant spectre, an afterburn. In suburbia, democracy and consumerism — twin pillars of life — have deep foundations. The beginning sentence of *Fall and Rise* in David Nobb's original novel, published in 1975, contains a reference to the "Heatwave".[4] A mood that might be accelerating Reggie's sacred disintegration: a meteorological event, of marsh miasma, presaged in an English Situationist

---

4   Before Nobbs developed the Perrin mythos, he had spent the 1960s as a jobbing gag writer for Frankie Howerd, *inter alia*. His first novel, *The Itinerant Lodger* (1965), also eerily touched on themes of *Rising Damp*, for obvious reasons.

of the same name, of which only two journals were ever published.[5]

The Situationist International, whose exhortation to "flee, but while fleeing, pick up a weapon", attenuated capitalist control in the urban landscape through the tactic of the *dérive*. Situationist Guy Debord's *Society of the Spectacle* and Ivan Chtcheglov's "Formulary for a New Urbanism" expose the banalisation of a capitalist onslaught that privatises both public and inner realm. Point taken. But a parochial surrealism is more attuned to the weird and horrific stains on the walls, or the magic front door, than the city's patterns. The domestic arsenal in *Home* provides the route out of the late twentieth century, forty years down the (train)line from Perrin.[6] The house, for Gerald, is key to a glacial pleroma that opens up time and space in the corridors and loft of his home, charting psychic reroutes to rebirth that the urban *dérive* can't reach. Like Reggie, a magician practicing invisibility in plain sight, Ballard's character Gerald projects an inner world onto the increasingly impossible geometries of the suburban house, as it begins to expand and contract, sensible to the real dualism of place and its dis/orientation: a breathing technology of exit, a dis-placement of the usual regimes of technology and magic,

---

5   The lyrics of the Sex Pistols' song "Holiday", also produced in 1976, fecundate a miasmic mood of summer heat.

6   It is no surprise that Gerald's "experiment" comes off the back of a road accident convalescence. Ballard's surrealist fusion of highway perversion and consumer desire, 1973's *Crash*, shine a motorway light on the vulcanised dissipation of the century. *Rising Damp*'s crawling wall patterns in this universe are equivalent to the patterns from car accident wounds: alternative sigils of modernity's dream world.

and two fingers to Dis Pater and other various chthonic lords. Such are the frustrations of Rigsby and Reggie: a lichen on modern housing systems, from the Dickensian to its modernist refreshment in conurbation. A delirious ideal of brown bricks, and grey mornings, with faces peering through curtains.

J.B. PRIESTLEY: Even our jokes have walls and hedges around them.

The sheer horror of the British wallowing in repetitious lines of houses, where the only recreation is to go to large consumer environments, is an illusion of sanitised anonymity, and withal gives service to the weird moments of the subsoil, from Machen's Brick Fields, to punk. An apparent nowhere fashioned as a DIY convenience retreat, Burroughs' 1970 feedback from the garden of "Eden" both picks up on the loss of innocence in the repeated patterns and pulses under the modern developments, (whilst channelising an unbridled jouissance of sex that metonymic "Eden" engenders, and contra any sex tape scandal designed to control life, *à propos* the Watergate Scandal) calling back the anonymous ennui of its promise. Burroughs' text was published in 1971 in England, after the 1970 German edition, and featured translations from French concrete and sound poet Henri Chopin, who lived in the Thames Estuary Leigh-on-Sea region of Essex, a few minutes' walk from where I grew up, and even closer to the main commuter station in that area. Such a cosmology is in constant search through the commute, the sacred geography of an existential audit.

Georges Bataille's secret society, Acéphale, formed in 1937, attempted to reintegrate the sacred into the twentieth century via the *chemin de fer*. Using the ancient sacrificial cults of antiquity as blueprint, the group met secretly in the Forest of Yveline, which in ancient times was called the Forest of Cruye, at a lightning-struck tree ringed by torchlight, as much as enforced secrecy. With the supposed *dénouement* of actual human sacrifice never realised, the group, with prominent members including Blanchot, Klossowski, Caillois and Leiris, disbanded their mystical communion after a few years. While it lasted, however, their arrival at the forest during these crepuscular assignations were structured with strict instructions from Bataille, which started with their arrival at the train station: "Do not acknowledge anyone, do not speak to anybody, find a seat away from the others," finally reaching "the place of the encounter". These instructions sound more like a guide to atomised contemporary commute than the group's Delphic theatrics, using the industrialised train system as transit to a space of unworkable unproductivity.

Reggie's gradual dissolution over many sitcom episodes of the work sphere is more effective, more gaudy in its magical intent, than Bataille's hermetic posturing. The necessary alchemic fluid of disappointment connects to the marsh's deeper code on Reggie's train tracks, mirroring the pilgrim's process of the travelling pageant wagon, and condensates *prima materia*, alchemical dew, on the train window as part of the "Great Work" and its landscape features: the mettle of man is tried in the furnace of humiliation. His plans for dissolution make him both a decadent artist and a scheming Machiavelli of the suburban, whose train travel is all the more redolent.

RUST IN URBE, the corroded city, the surrealist curse, seen as graffiti from the train line.[7]

C-L: Thank you Reggie. Er, all those names, they were a sort of... middle-management test?
REGGIE: Oh yes, of course, you didn't realise? Yes, yes. It's the latest thing — 'industrial psychology'. Try it on the Germans!
C-L: Yes, I will!
REGGIE: Well, you must go. Nice to see you again, and good luck with the Exotic Ices, you slimy creep.

Reggie's ability to throw his work colleagues off track is a weaponising of discomfort through the disjuncture that is humour's special brew. In the world of globalised commerce lies the incipient evidence of what is now dogma: things can be bad, but must be rendered positive in an ego-driven rhetoric of positivity. Comedy has little to do with this enforced positivity, but operates more as a distortion of heterogenous and personalised environments. Repeated in old videotape, the 1970s retain the crease of a globalised mysticism that Reggie is attuning to. The "weapon" of Perrin's English shamanism lies in demarcating ludic vacuoles of unknowing, liver spots of the *genius loci*.

---

7   The return commute of modernity is caparisoned with arcane magic in M.R. James' "Casting the Runes" (1911). Mr Dunning, a specialist in alchemy, espies prophetic news in the apparition of a death notice within the commercial glass planes of a London electric tram.

Noise 2

Monopoleigh was capricious by sinister indoor sheds... The Holsten dream of a man with net curtains... pacing out local boozers, in ludic board game crawl...

Extra-Parochial

Denoting those areas outside the delineated jurisdiction of the civil or ecclesiastical parish, *extra-parochial* areas operate like blind spots within a mundane locale, like that of the suburban sphere.[8]

These zones represented a legal nuisance, exempt from usual administrational control, which is no doubt why they were abolished in 1857 with the Extra-Parochial Places Act. This saw parishes amalgamated to adjoining civil boundaries, or indeed gaining certified independent status as civil parishes.

Parishes insufflate and deflates according to the dualistic territorialisations of land ownership and decree. Such an approach can be matched in the 1860 Union of Benefices Act, which sought to combine the extant churches of the City of London to large parishes, thereby freeing up space for commercial expansion.

Effectively dis-placements, famous examples of erstwhile extra-parochial sites were, tellingly, Nowhere in Norfolk, Nomansland in Devon and No Man's Heath in Warwickshire (Where did you set *Rising Damp*? Nowhere...). Not only were these advantageous sites for non-conformist religious gatherings, making one think of the Diggers and Ranters of the English Civil War, but they now function as a model for the underside of the parochial, or indeed industrially, the suburban. Such affordances spread into a wide menu of cultural fields, but it is specifically the British sitcom and its occult correspondences as iterations of the marsh's substratum that are at their most powerful when drawing on this specifically regional modality of delimited exigency.

---

8   *Speak, Rainaldus!*

REGGIE: There will be two marketing areas. David will be in control of Hertfordshire, and Tony in charge of East Lancashire.

At Sunshine Desserts, and in a willing unravelling of sense, Reggie draws an outline on geographical maps for marketing outlined with a bin and a handbag, "chosen from the computer with data fed in from the tasting". Psychogeographic strategy using everyday items (*Essex, may it fall of the map!...*)

DAVID: 20% of my area seems to be in the sea.
REGGIE: We are trying to reach the trawler market.

The parochial itself, under the jurisdiction of the desk-bound Parish Clerk, beats the bounds of a small landscape. The rogation ceremony, known in the Lutheran tradition as Rogate Sunday, practiced regularly in CofE parishes until the 1960s,[9] saw the congregation ritually demarcate the parish boundaries with walk and prayer to fend off wheat rust. As much a Pagan hangover, it is also a circumscription of what lay outside the extra-parochial. Small-scale pilgrimages were both remembrances of an earth-based seasonal-pseudo-Paganism to church practices, a libation in miniature pilgrimage and song literally to the soil, trampling down ears of corn in the harvest sunlight, charging the fields with cartographic understanding. This practice can also be attributed to the mystery plays — a tethering of the spiritual universe to specific British towns and cities, as much as to certain key points in the country's commercial and metaphysical mappemonde.

The magical form of the touring mystery play, the rogation

---

9   My grandfather, organist of Great Stambridge Parish, used to conduct a
      rogation ceremony around the field of Essex with a portable organ.

ceremony, the commute, all make geography sacred and confound the easy duality of nowhere and somewhere at the level of the comedically mysterious. This piercing of the hole, the dilation tactic of an odd circumscribed locality confounds the anaemic notion of the site-specific for the dark laughter track of a *détourned* local history. The extra-parochial is the opposite of the demiurgic ersatz nowhere: the zenith and nadir of dis-orientation's poles, although both predate, co-exit and foretell zones of hyper-capital. Suburbia confounds geographical specificity and place-lessness. *When you are nowhere physically, you are everywhere spiritually*: in the duality of the *Cloud of Forgetting* and the *Cloud of Unknowing*, one is everywhere and nowhere at once — the gnostical dis-orientation inherent to the marsh finds its darkest conation here. Despite myth being predetermined on the availability of modes of whatever present you find yourself haplessly in, the extra-parochial within deep locales belies a suburban life reduced to the hermeneutics of domestic, and the local as negative. The negative theology, or apophatic mysticism, detailed in *The Cloud of Unknowing*, resolves the inevitable localism inherent to myth. In modernity, this localism is eschewed for the globalised universality of general unlocated parity. The vacuole of the unthought extra-parochial models this threshold elucidated by Bataille's notion of "absence of myth" for the 1970s, but also allows it to travel through ages, and the fields.

Noise 3

Enigmatic cleric's script, swiped across mud clumps… plotting moments of etiolated surrealism and saving it as Fortean logic: Add Fr. Rolfe, as required… "History happens so rarely now; I mean, its scattered all over the place…". Archaeological remains make a lot of noise. Herodotus: Get fucked.

Trowel and Error

Antiquarian's Logick

"Turning in an anti-clockwise direction around the Essex Running well [...] will cause an "evil" or "negative" result [...] as a form of invocation!".

Two ludic instances of what I am calling "supernatural archaeology" divest the spectral patina of a site. The two sites to illuminate the extra-parochialist pulp interstices of sacred and profane geography are the Running Well, in Essex, and a so-called ritual spring in Llgadwy, immortalsied by an episode of the erstwhile Channel 4 TV archaeology romp *Time Team*. Where St Winefride's Well, frequented by Fr. Rolfe, occasioned a unique series of pilgrimage de(sur)facements, these wells also mobilise a supernatural relationship to digging up the past abetted by dose of Antiquarian fabulation.

The Essex Running Well, located in an ignominious ditch, came to the attention of the reading public in the 1980s, in occult researcher Andrew Collins' 1983 self-published tract *The Running Well Mystery*, where it etymologically links the name to both "running" (water) and "rune" (mystery).[1] A

---

1   My role as reporter at *The Leigh & Westcliff Times* newspaper has a
     link to said author Collins that goes beyond the auto-theoretical

book that also details his investigations into Earth mystery practices, which saw a largely tabloid-driven revival in the United Kingdom at this time, in relation to nefarious pagan goings on, ranging from sacrifices of hares to video nasties.[2]

Place-based mythemes of somewhere like Runwell run a litter of allusions, re-mobilised continually in the present: disparate hermetic and personal fragments and cosmologies attached to sites, proof of heretical affiliation to the original Gnostics' apocryphal method of fabulation. The second-century cleric Irenaeus complains of the Christian heretic group "putting forth their own compositions [...] every one of them generates something new every day, according to his ability; for no-one is truly accepted amongst them unless

---

effectiveness of bringing one's paid employment into the texture of research: namely, the fact that Collins was employed in my role at the same newspaper thirty years previous, which is more than a proliferating coincidence of comedy occulture. He writes on page 19 of *The Black Alchemist*: "Leaving my duties as a sales representative and writer for the *Leigh Times* newspaper for a few minutes, I decided to phone Bernard. Cruising the streets of Leigh-on-Sea, I glanced out across the Thames Estuary from Essex to Kent. From a call box outside the main post office, I called the psychic [...] 'Do you know of a Sussex village called Wilmington?' he asked, concluding his story. 'I think there's a priory there with a crypt.' As I tried to scribble a few notes, I thought for a moment. Wasn't that the name of the Sussex village in *Dad's Army*, the TV comedy series about a battalion of Home Guard volunteers during the Second World War? No, hold on, that was Warmington-on-Sea!"

2   This was in benign terms *pace* Collins, but also in ostensibly sinister forms with the English Underground in groups like Psychic TV's false implication in a video nasty scandal.

he develops some enormous fictions". Bataille, being one of the most prominent philosophers of the twentieth century to reinvigorate an interest in the Gnostic material, repurposed their strict duality of body and spirit with the inversion of base matter. With a dubious antiquarian approach, this melding of fiction and the soiled of the locale uses a radical contingency. Such "Antiquarian's Logic", as Collins terms a chapter in his book, is read through their hermetic hermeneutics — or herme(neu)tics: a neologism explicitly locating the occult and synchronic fictional basis to textual transmission and interpretation, as much as a mouldy texture to historicism.

The fantastical daydreams of Reggie Perrin, that are at best disjunctive and necessary for the sitcom's strange rhythm, are cut-away visions, tools for seeing his future, fantastical asides as he stares into the middle distance, refracted through lurid colourings of the sitcom's filming: measured as a similarly Gnostic heresy against the pattern of the normal episode. Fears and fantasies as fictions that come to pass are played out in surreal tableaux, only in front of his eyelids. His office desk will be hallucinated into a field, with the torrid scene of him and his secretary Joan sprawled thereon. Or C.J., played with hysterical pomp by John Barron, will be transformed into a folk horror rabbit, or Frankenstein, before the scene cuts back to "reality".

Reality, even with the severance into alienation with the first cuneiform cut, is unclear. An Antiquarian's Logic is the fount of a great deal of the droves and romances surrounding Runwell. The collage of myth and fact surrounding it suggest the location has existed since the earliest recorded date of AD 939, but ancient sites, like the cut-up, alter the future, to let "fiction" seep through. The fictions that are the backbone of the Running Well's story, as Collins confirms, are the writings of a Victorian folklorist and Rector of Runwell Parish, John Edward Bazille-Corbin, who was instituted in 1923, and wrote *Runwell St Mary — A popular account of the parish, its Running Well, its Church and its Clergy, together with some local legends and various notes* in 1942, the authority of which Collins himself belies: "It was almost certainly he who generated a local interest in the church's superstitions. Indeed, some even suggested that he'd concocted them to draw attention and popularity to the church!"[3]

Generations of such antiquarians are the sham historians who also "salt" the spring in the 2008 *Time Team* episode, which takes Robinson and pals to Llgadwy in Powys: a serious archaeological folly. Where incongruous objects are found in a manufactured "ritual spring"; a megalithic stone is found to be too shallow in the earth to be genuine; carved heads huddle near the well; and an Iron Age "La Tène" sword is deduced to be a "real relic" from a "sham site" when it is found stratified in mud *over* a piece of barbed wire from the late 1990s. But the relics uncovered in both instances of TV reliquary could be a collage of the arcane and the modernist Antiquarian's Logic: impacted in the mud of the shitty spring are "real" relics interred to deliberately cheat the linear patterns of the past and let the fiction seep through — such as the accounts from the Runwell Rector also effect. The relics embody the temporal slippage of reality for Reggie. Archaeologists talk much of the importance of such disrupted context in a site's material, which is owed to the practice of local autodidacts working, evidently, according to Antiquarian's Logic however spurious and patently illegal their activity. If this is the post-

3 In 2017, Collins and I, with three friends, visited the Running Well in his Peugeot 206.

modern enlisting of "strange old aesthetic objects", it is pre-empted by the incomplete, local, unorthodox base of this knowledge as productive, but also humorous: the church leaflet and local paper syndrome of geographical specificity,

Tony Robinson.

as much as a prioritising of the made over the given.

In *Time Team*'s Welsh site, inscription is also of the essence. "Ancient" marks are also scratched through the surface discoloration of a small statue found in the artificial sacred spring, meaning they must have been added much later, a truly anachronistic patina of damp, de(sur)facing marks of time travel. Layers of mud or the fluvial cut of the well lead us to both the medieval period and the 1970s at once, a hilarious collision of Essex bombast, self-promotion, suburban ennui and the torrid dreams of Roman decadence. Unwittingly, sham archaeologist rectors create a perfect blueprint of Mud Flat Time; these antiquarian poseurs, no doubt influenced by the increased Victorian knowledge of the Holy Land and the strata of biblical history — it was Revd Edward Hincks who untimely deciphered Ancient Mesopotamian cuneiform for the first time in 1857 — have succeeded in exposing the *différance* of site, the weird incretion of Damp's Code implicit in the (sediment of the) present.

TONY ROBINSON: If we look at the stratigraphy, we've just about reached the 1970s.

The marshland as expanded mythic zone is focused in these two archaic examples into a channelled place for ritual gesture and pulp conceit for Reggie to draw on. An essential function of the unconscious in the artistic process: the godless combination of modernism and Mystical index of the subliminal in the activities of the mind, symbolised in Meister Eckhart's *fundus animae*. When the medieval mystic Eckhart appropriated this term, he linked the notion to the metaphoric geography of a well, from the biblical spring of living water, and the good soil in the parable of the sower, synonymous in concept due to an evocation of depth: the releasing of a mystic blockage of the subject, previously trapped in the homogenous world.

Collins cites the Running Well as a "deep elliptical hole", and links Runwell's hellish associations pursuant of the ever proverbial "hell hole". The "Legend of the Devil's Claw" as it is attached to the local parish is a tale befitting or even outdoing antiquarian M.R. James. Parishioners witness the devil issuing from the sermonising incumbent Rainaldus one Sunday in the 1500s, as he is chased around the church with his dark master on his heels. The only trace found of Rainaldus after his exit through the south porch is a "bubbling hissing pool of liquid" on the floor which became "a circular black stain". Such a mark is epitomic of place's stain, or *tache aveugle* (dirty smear), the vacuole of the extra-parochial as the widening gyre of time that Antiquarian Logic helps uncover. Where Reginald Perrin's absurdist tactics are an exit from existence, for a route out of homogeneity — the demarcation of the Parochial Zone locates these performances, recalls the aberrant "nowhere" — a funnel down into disrupted strata. The weirdly stilted vicar in the 1972 adaptation of *A Warning to the Curious* talks to Peter Vaughan about his battle with occult lore in the parish, owing to his lack of "localness":

> *VICAR: Most of my parishioners take these* [folklore] *traditions more seriously than their churchgoing. Fascinating… for the historian or the antiquarian perhaps. But uphill work for the vicar. I'm not really a native you see; I've only lived here twenty years. I sometimes wonder what my role here is. I'm certainly not a Father Confessor.*

These atmospheres, in turn, are transmitted by modern systems of technology, such as the adaptation herewith, progeniture of the TV archaeologist. Archaeology's broadcastability itself, exemplified in the ludic aberrancy of *Time Team*, has provided soiled prime-time riposte to the Situationist tactic of unearthing paving stones. Mortimer Wheeler — "the embodiment of popular archaeology through the medium of television" — finds a Y2K iteration in Tony Robinson. Although the landscape of the sitcom so far has shown that TV itself is a uniquely archaeological medium itself, without the mediation of a presenter. Digging and damp are inextricable: archaeology as an unfolding practice "found" ancient cuneiform, but it also recursively exposes itself as a uniquely mid-century modality in its technological popularity.

The digging in *A Warning to the Curious* reveals furrows uniquely contemporary to the time of the adaptation's making. Disruption in the mud is an effect of time's disturbance, traced for us in damp. Not only does Damp's Code precede the advent of sitcom as broadcast medium, but in superseding time like the alchemist's mettle, the transmission of motile geology, which blends deep time with video fuzz, foregrounds disturbance, or the cut-up of the signal, as the dissonance of the trowel unearthing the past into the present.

Technics of the twentieth and twenty-first century index this disturbance in and through both television and radar technology. In archaeological geophysics, this is demonstrable in the black-and-white pixels of noise thrown up as the presence of resistance across a landscape territory survey. Geophysics picks up disturbance in the layers of mud as the TV affectively picks up ancient voices from the marsh, with both drawing on the same technological methods of reassembling signal into image. The 1970s bring the technological medium of tape, radar, signal and its reflexive occulture into comedy as the laugh tracks of a muddy trench. I'll go further: *Time Team* is a sitcom itself, and why not? It follows the same structure each week, inhabited by the same characters who always wear the same clothes, to boot — like TV personae, with recognisable accessories, catchphrase and roles.

Rising Damp itself is, of course, page 1 of TV as supernatural archaeology. Where the sitcom is a machine for subverting time, sensible to the systems of ancient and modern technics nesting in upon themselves, TV logistics practice magic in plain sight, blurring, like the white lines on a VHS, the distinction between archaeology and television.

Rising Damp, and *The Fall and Rise of Reginald Perrin*, evidently antiquated sitcom models, also circumnavigate this particular ooze of routine through an excavation of the experience of repeats — surely, we all know these sitcoms either through old hashed-up VHS or through internet viewings. This is something contingent on the present, not on the moment of original space-time broadcast: an antiquarian's radical contingency. Outside the sitcoms diegetic course (if there is such a space), the once-loathed portal site of Reggie's offices used as location in the sitcom were recently bulldozed, with the results posted up on a fan streaming site, or on YouTube's media graveyard. A nesting of analogue and digital affects.

 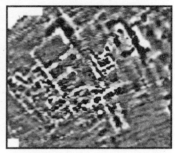

Ceremonial landscapes make a lot of noise: TV static vs geophysical archaeological survey.

Perhaps the contingency of the repeat is inscribed within damp itself: an available mode despite and in the present indeed because of its repetition, all the more apparent in the post-industrial fold-in of degraded digital iterations and poor screen grabs. The repeated inscription of the same filed movements and utterances accrue weight with age, but are vulnerable to disembowelment by the consumerism of endless empty instants. With the odd VHS — whose colours fades with blurry white lines like an old photocopied page — the remaining episodes have been watched thus. Their existence is indurate to self-satisfied gluttony of digital box sets, because even in this most apparently cosy scene, surety is unseated. Rainaldus, Corbin, Collins, Robinson concur a method used by Perrin in his spurious inventing of paratextual fictions that stretch across media, text and texture: Trowel and Error.

REGGIE: I like to stroke my nipple with strawberry and lichee ripple.

Noise 4

Dogends of the Nag Hammadi... plus fun-machine-gabbery: live from The Crucible... One feels that the dry sherries are taking their toll on the Ladies' Darts Championships... Should I be drinking at 6 pm on a Wednesday question mark... Leaning on props that are rotten?

The Pub's Alchemic Accelerationism

Reginald Perrin's drunken speech on *the role of luxury desserts in a competitive industrial society* at a seminar at Bilberry Hall (the home of the British Fruit Association) is titled by boss C.J., "Are We Getting Our Just Desserts?"

REGGIE: Thank you. Thank you very much indeed. Thank you, Mister... whatever your name is. When my boss said to me "Reginald Iolanthe Perrin, you are a senior sales earwig at Sunshine Desserts, and they are holding a seminar on instant puddings at Bilberry Hall, and I want you to talk on 'Are We Getting Our Just Desserts?'", my first thought was: "What a pathetic title for a talk!" (C.J. scowls). But then I thought again (C.J. loses his scowl). My second thought was: "What a pathetic title for a talk!" (C.J. finds his scowl again). But I come here anyway because I have something very important to say to you all. We are told that we need more growth: 6% per year. More chemicals to cure more pollution, caused by more chemicals. More car parks for more tourists who want to get away from more car parks. More food, to make us more fat, to make us use more slimming aids, to make us take more pills, to make us ill, to make us take more pills, to make more profit. More boring speakers, making more boring speeches, at more boring conferences.

DR HUMP: (mutters to Mr Watkins): This is rubbish. (Reggie overhears).

REGGIE: More rubbish, that's a very good point, thank you Hump. But what has all this growth done for me? Well, I'll tell you. One day I'll die, and on my grave, it will say: "Here lies Reginald Iolanthe Perrin. He didn't know the names of the trees and the flowers, but he knew the rhubarb crumble sales figures for Schleswig Holstein." [Holsten? ed.]

Filmmaker and surrealist Humphrey Jennings' book *Pandaemonium, 1660–1886: The Coming of the Machine as Seen by Contemporary Observers* collated a vision of early modernity in textual accounts that he envisaged as "knots in a great net of tangled time and space — the moments at which the situation of humanity is clear — even if only for the flash time of the photographer or the lightning". Likewise, the speech represents a moment of clarity for Reggie, aided by wine. Jennings' pop fragments chart responses to technological speed and industry through descriptions of landscapes and hellish machines. Reggie Perrin's disastrous Bilberry Hall seminar speech ranks as a viable observation for Jennings' collation, a noteworthy "knot" found in Reggie's relentless "industrial psychology" jokes as caustic critique of shit Britain's granular control of mind and body. Perhaps these reflexive fragments are the only route we have open to us. It is no doubt what Reggie feels after he's bitten into industrialisation and found out what it is made of. His knots of revelation need tethering to landscapes, even if that means a series of rapidly changing scenes like those seen out of the train commute window.

For Jennings, the early Industrial Revolution's augural furnaces re-wrote labourers' psychic attachment to tools and landscape. As in Blake's satanic mills, the restoration-period *Paradise Lost* referenced in the book's title takes on a baroque carbolic horror, sensing the nascent transductive shift between humans and technology at the level of devilment: demons building the city, lit by the flames of forges, rise up from hell, to speed our transit to Reggie's "tough world of the blancmange".

Jennings' collage of technology, in its disorienting iterations through the centuries, captures the hallucinatory quality of increasingly de-materialised sites: landscapes changed by speed. Still, geological drift and the derangement of the senses are cosmic metaphor for local erasure. Reggie's incantation is apotropaic magic for regional re-enchantment. Jennings reminds us all of this parochial loss through the scorch marks of industry's effects, and asks:

"In what sense have the Means of Vision kept pace with these alterations [of the machine age]? I am referring not to the Arts as a commodity for Bond Street, or as a piece of snobbery in Mayfair, or as a means of propaganda in Bloomsbury, or as a method of escapism in Hampstead... but to the Means of Vision by which "the emotional side of our nature" is kept alive and satisfied and fed — our nature as Human Beings in the anthracite drifts of South Wales, in the cotton belt of Lancashire, in the forges of Motherwell — how the emotional side of their nature has been used, altered, tempered, appealed to in these two hundred years."

Fermented metal is the skeleton of all epochs, but Milton's invocation of the seething building of Hell, signalling through the flames, is an appropriately hellish scene for the apparent incontrovertibility of globalisation's inscription and erasing of the parochial, and its glimmer of vision. Blake equally heralds the Gnostic melee of these spiritual materials, a new form of this "Means of Vision" that sees the biblical Hell as both the genesis and future project of capitalism, particularly when it plots up in England's fields: in Blake's printmaking, Vision's patina, like time's damp, is dependent on, and constitutive of, his metal printmaking substrates, and upon a calling down to earth of mythological place into the recognisable cartographies of London.

The hieroglyphic strangeness of the "Great Work" of sixteenth- and seventeenth-century hermetic alchemy relies on the fiery blasting of furnaces and the transmutation of gold for its interpolation of human and mineral. A radical technology of the time, alchemy was not just a metallurgy of pots and alembics, but a spiritual journey through substance. Such an operation has seen the marsh landscape materialised as the symbolic and real substratum of the sitcom in Part 1: *Rising Damp*, elaborated as a technological alchemisation of landscape. The process of transmuting material to achieve the "Philosopher's Stone" sees internal landscapes mirrored in *prima materia*: material analogue to rewinding spiritual degradation through the quickened end of base matter. In the words of religious scholar Mircea Eliade, "On the mineral level of existence, the stone [in alchemy] was realising this miracle: it eliminated the interval of time which separated the present condition of an "imperfect" (crude) metal from its final condition (when it would become gold). The Stone achieved transmutation almost instantaneously: *it superseded Time*."

The process of alchemy is an experiment in accelerating time, fast-forwarding materiality, as much as it rewinds the psychic state. The forges of Britain, and the fire and industry turbocharged in the Industrial Revolution, later funnelled into making instant pudding for neoliberal jobs, finds in alchemy's industrial cousin, metallurgy, this equivalent processual metaphor for Reggie Perrin in the ersatz office. Metallurgy repeatedly charges numerous landscapes of action, from Mesopotamian ritual to the hyperindustrial.

Accelerationism, named a twentieth-century "political heresy", designates a nihilistic alignment in philosophical thought. The excesses of capitalist culture and its remedy are found in the speeding up and intensifying of the latter's tendencies, one of which is the dislocation from the spatial virtual networks. The at-once generative but homogenising affordances of technology's machinic deterritorialisation seem to echo metallurgic technology.

> *BERNARD STIEGLER: In originary disorientation, this differential of forces-as-potential is the difference of rhythms between human beings and organised inorganic being (technics), as well as the de-phasing brought about by technics' structural advancement, in its differentiation, on the living being it constitutes and differentiates by bringing it into being.*

A mythotechnesis — the comodulating of human operations, technology and cosmological action in this alchemic form of accelerationism — is a travelling backward and forwards in time, changing the human, and constituting it. The furnaces of this epoch's psyche get especially fired up as a new relationship to production. Something is demonic in the metallurgic ores of incipient globalisation: not just in this fabled "coming of the machine" but as one instance of a continually metastable frequency of *Code: Damp*. Charting a disorienting route through human consciousness, from science's hazy birth in magic, stoked up in the *Pandeamonium* of the Industrial Revolution, whose horrors in technological advance also ran a disorienting arrangement and rearrangement of the senses. Relaying and re-recording over previous imbrications, a tape of technological consciousness. Mark Fisher, in his text on this relationship, confirms this duality: "1. Everyone is an accelerationist 2. Accelerationism has never happened."

Where *Time Team*'s sacred spring exposed the working of local antiquarians as supernatural archaeology, another episode elucidates the workings of this alchemical accelerationism in the causes of Reggie's misery. Series 9, Episode 5, "The Blast Furnace in the Cellar", unfolds in a pub car park near Iron Bridge, a valley that doubles as birth canal of the British Industrial Revolution. "The Mill at Leighton (formerly The Kynnersley Arms) is a family-friendly village pub situated between Ironbridge and Shrewsbury, on the B4380."

REGGIE: More car parks for more tourists who want to get away from more car parks.

Unearthing the remains of a seventeenth-century blast furnace for smelting iron, *Time Team* deftly scry Shropshire's Enlightenment with the help of resident TV archaeometallurgist Gerry McDonnell and industrial archaeologist Rob Kinchin-Smith. *Time Team*'s pub car park hermeneutics is magic thinking, recalled in the huge cuneiform de(sur)facement graffito in Baghdad's Al-Sinak multi-storey car park. It all makes some kind of terrible sense. *Of course,* a pub would be opened on top of a furnace. The remains of industrial archaeology leave parch marks in the grass — that reveal buried archaeological sites — also mark being parched, prior to entry. A spectral rekindling of the Means of Vision through the carousing communality of other dimensions.

George Orwell's article on the ideal boozer, "The Moon Under Water", tells us about the loss of the pub and the ideal conditions in this most fantastical of creative zones. In the contemporary, this destitution results from soaring rents, the smoking ban, the degradation of the career barman, the moribund cocktail bars, the internet, Netflix, the bastard brewery tie-ins. Orwell was in 1946 imagining a convivial yet particular atmosphere, based on the fact that pubs are special places in technology's pre-history. A line is traced in popular memory through the zone of the pub, as the site for recursive appearance of the empirically eerie, in characters, acts and comedic traces of self-reconnaissance. Take Rik Mayall, for instance, who shimmers into recognition as an extra in the film *American Werewolf in London* in the infamous pub scene: metonym to parochial unfriendliness, before immortalising the ultimate shit pub in BBC sitcom *Bottom*. Dick Head, the landlord in *Bottom*, might be a complete and utter bastard, but the pub is still jam-packed full of archaeology, as AD 1974's *Libidinal Economy*, written by Lyotard, suggests.

Lyotard maintains that the proletariat was complicit in the apparently anodyne funnelling of free time into the boozer, the subordinated desire and subjection to consumer territories of spaces of life and entertainment, eschewing a pre-industrial rurality for the bonhomie of the capitalist pub. Mark Fisher in his essay riffing thereon, asks: "*Hands up who wants to give up their anonymous suburbs and pubs and return to the organic mud of the peasantry?*" The answer, for Reggie, is you don't have to choose! The mephitic mud of the marshy Akkadian brickfields is the underlining ghastliness of suburbia, *pace* Machen. Mark's critique of accelerationism rightly detests the flaccid embourgeoisement of politics *qua* career sandbagging – the "[writing] papers about antagonism, then all off to the pub afterwards". But there is something crucial about the pub as an essential site of generative negativity and activity. Sherds of historical memory are *forged* in the pub. The pub allows access to other domains. Arnold, the narrator of *N* (1936) by Arthur Machen, is talking to friends in a corner of a tavern in(n) in London, and tells the gathered: "I believe that there is a perichoresis, an interpenetration. It is possible, indeed, that we three are now sitting among desolate rocks, by bitter streams... And with what companions?"

Writing in Akkadian that says *The Odd Lager* is found on a stone under the car park, a transgenerational script reckoned with by Rigsby and Reggie. When Reggie returns in disguise after his perceived death, his first port of call is the work boozer, where he sits near his colleagues, hubristically listening to their chatter. There might be objects cast in this bog of surmise. Rigsby might not leave the confines of his damp house with its litany of lodgers, but this is because he has his very own special brew of tenants.

Tony Robinson: I get blinkered vision when looking at a furnace. How do they manage it?

The disporting melee of furnace, locality and vision is capitulated by an example of technology.

The split-screen revolution in televised darts founds another alchemic accelerationism of the pub.

The ultimate Pub Olympics — *The Indoor League*, broadcast on ITV from 1973 to 1977, alongside *Rising Damp* — darts on TV engages in a magical dissonance of reality that conjures this unique force.

George Orwell: Games are only played in the public bar, so that in the other bars you can walk about without constantly ducking to avoid flying darts.

Prior to the 1970s, it had been virtually impossible to capture on the TV screen the darter's reaction and the thud of impact on the board of the arrow, but the split-screen effect surfaced this blind spot, as a visual cut-up.

Dart Ja Vu: Essex man Bobby George in split-screen.

Producer Nick Hunter explained:

NICK: Darts was being covered largely with too many close-ups of the board, while the player, out of shot, was throwing the dart. Because I was just cutting backwards and forwards, and I was wondering how on earth I could stop this cutting. There were viewers complaining. You know in your bones it's not working very well. So, we had a bit of a meeting and in the end a cameraman said, "Well, why don't you split the screen?"

And on the split-screen, you can see the face, you can see the board, and it made all the difference. It made it easier to cover, and better to cover at the same time, which is quite rare.

100!

You could watch a player start to lose it.

60!

Or the opposite, if you like.

You could watch a player gradually realising he's getting in control of the match, and that's a precious part of that split-screen.

The alchemy of editing to "supersede time" is a darts cut-up to "let's the future leak out". The constant "cutting" he describes is surely not dissimilar to the cut-up of magical tape interference.

Burroughs has always cautioned against atavism in magical practice: alchemists would be using the most "up to date" technology at hand, he said. The cut-up, and the sigil, as magical technologies of the self, were used as a practice of transformation to interpolate image production and control that the TV represented, by Thee Temple ov Psychick Youth (TOPY) in the late 1980s. This ritual magick collective, founded by Genesis P-Orridge of Throbbing Gristle fame, extended the cut-up idea into television editing, at a time when the VHS was itself becoming a personal editing tool: cutting up and opening the TV schedules to a new form of popular mnemonic device.[4] P-Orridge's association in the video nasty scandals of the early 1980s (a topic equally pilloried and glorified in an episode of *The Young Ones* in 1984) underline the role of the Grand Master editor who creates a version of reality. TOPY state: "*This could be used as a modern alchemical allegory* [...] *The editor actually has more REAL control over the version you see than any other person involved in the production. Editing is a form of BIAS. Only a Master can edit it all so it makes sense to a viewer later on.*"

Corroborating the metallurgical weft of the pub scene and its technological mediation, this details the difference between cut and split. The apparent randomness of the darts hitting

---

4   Gerald and Reggie's acts of defiance, as much as the lettering of the
      subtitles are ludic strategies to counter control more frequently associated
      with formally signed-up representatives of occulture.

the board is another occult measurement. Tony Robison suggests that, in a *Time Team* dig occurring in the "middle of a housing estate" where modern facilities prevent much deep digging, putting random test pits in is "a bit like chucking darts at a dart board". Such a technique also recalls Reggie drawing outlines for sales areas on a map with a bin and a handbag. An apparently aleatory method of radical contingency is crucial to the pub's dual effect of local and cosmic.

DARTS COMMENTATOR: Not only is he not in the same league, he's not in the same parish.

Chuckle Brother: Ripped a history out of reverse psychology.

Northern pub comic and music hall inheritor Charlie Chuck

espouses such chance methods with his *Chuckoscope*, in a late-night episode of *The James Whale Show* from the ITV Network.

> *CHUCK: Behind me is an ancient alternative zodiac found in a cave in the eighteenth century by a man called Dave. Here in Wakefield, it might not mean a lot to you, it means even less to me [...] It took me many years and a lot of studying to find out about the Esoteric meanderings of an ancient culture.[5]*

Like Reggie, Chuck's avowedly "industrial psychology" jokes combine uncanny music hall or even Mumming play glamour with the an antiquarian's herme(neu)tics of time to travel — both in the colliding of technical layers, and in scrying through his horoscope's shitty capitalist icons. A surreal end-of-the-pier charlatanism, evinced in Sid Waddell AKA *The Voice of Darts*. Waddell dug deep into ancient reference, a popular intellectual, tuning in to the arcane code of darts' mercurial *mise-en-scène*.

> *WADDELL: The atmosphere — a cross between the Munich beer festival and the Coliseum — when the Christians were on the menu. There was less noise when Pompeii was swamped in lava!*

---

5   Tools of divination, operating through damp's code, mutate, pop up like marsh parasites across space-time. J.G. Ballard attempted to update the tools of the augur with his 1978 story *Zodiac 2000*: "The houses of our psychological sky are no longer tenanted by rams, goats and crabs but by helicopters, cruise missiles and intra-uterine coils, and by all the spectres of the psychiatric ward". The "kind of farm animal" that the hepatoscopists sacrificed for their entrail scriptures find their counterpart in the machines which guard and shape our lives in so many ways — above all, the "Taurean computer, seeding its limitless possibilities".

This Gnostic decadence of the Roman world within the pub recalls Frankie Howerd's corralling of prophetic forces and innuendo, mixed with the gauche sports commentary of Alan Partridge. Both Chuck and Wadell tessellate pub culture onto an "ancient alternative" mystical practice through TV, as seen in Part 1. Post-Enlightenment, post-globalisation, pre-cuneiform.

Divination is perhaps common to alehouses as, speaking in a thirteen-day trance from a London "Ordinary" (an old term for an alehouse), religious radical Anna Trapnell undergoes another kind of prophesy in 1654. In lieu of the Dictaphone as a technological recorder, the lengthy revelation is transcribed "live" onto paper by an anonymous character (lost to history) called "the Relator" and published as *The Cry of a Stone*.

Trapnell is part of the Millenarian tumult of the English Civil War, as much a radical as the proto-communist Ranters and Diggers who levelled up from the unquiet earth of the 1640s. Trapnell's "Ordinary" prophecy is tunnelled from gut into beer condensation: a "cry of a stone" is perhaps a different kind of pub rock to Dr. Feelgood's, and it is the "entrails of scripture" from which she prophesises, recalling the divinatory hermeneutics of the sheep's liver. With the "entrails", Trapnell is knowingly referencing this ancient practice of the hepatoscopoi, also suggesting that she too can foretell the future through ancient exegesis as corporeal matter: biblical hermeneutics in offal.

The title is an allusion to Chapter 2, Verse 11 of the biblical book of Habakkuk: "For the stone shall cry out of the wall and the beam out of the timber shall answer it — All things have a voice". Whereas Trapnell foregrounds the Second Coming of Christ with her title, as was the wont of Fifth

Monarchists, the resultant divinatory gnosis also comes from her *being the stone:* she is the sediment, the damp, from which the prophesy is mapped, reminiscent of the metallurgical ores of the alchemical furnace: a contamination of human and technics, at an organological level.

The trance and its words digress in register: veering between Trapnell's biographical details and mystical exegesis, it predates a post-structuralist erosion of authorial agency, evoking both the local historian and earlier, the heresy of the Gnostics — masticators, confabulators and spewers of sources. Trapnell, in her prophesying, does not own the text: she is a channeller, making the re-enactment an arcane substrate activated in her and then our "present". In Trapnell's re-enactment, the Holy Lands are "live" in a pub in central London in 1654. The past indeed runs back and forth through the text as much as the prophesying itself, that constitute a mode of oratorical political autobiography as much as a version of post-Reformation pulp mysticism.

HOUSE MOTHER NORMAL: My idea of a holiday was never the sea anyway. On those pub outings, all they were interested in was the insides of the pubs along the front at Southend, one after the other. They went into the first, next to the coach park, and so it went on, all along the front. The Kursaal bored me, but all the men used to love it when the pubs were shut.

This combining of the quotidian and the strange is a galvanising comedic force that both propagates and undermines modern life. Contingent transformation to lived moments, pub prophesy confronts Flat Time with the force of a hyperindustrial yet archaic mysticism. No time is better spent wasted than in the pub, whose substratum sits with duration in discomfort, and the metaphoric and material superseding of time. The pub as a place for mummers, darts players,[6] mystical divination, is lined by *the Blast Furnace in the Cellar*. The crucial Inns and Outs of popular culture forge a knowledge creation that transcends genre.

The well and the furnace that headed these archaeological discourses, as comodulations of elemental forms and human purpose, weird incursion into the landscape, are instances of what Charlie Chuck's esoteric comedy, as a function, opens out onto. Like sacred springs, whose central dilation tactic of the swirling whirlpool opens a widening gyre of space-time, the furnace under the pub is a point of intensity for the pub's generation into a creative communion. A specific historic and ritual place stores unfileable[7] documents of both telluric, fluvial and human flow. What a blast.

---

6   What about us? (Littler!)

7   This "unfileable" nature will also be related directly to the filing systems and bureaucracy of the mid-century office workspace and its unworking through damp.

Southend Seafront.

Noise 5

The russet of Granada TV seeps in to the resolve of the building... Good reception, although smeared test card.

Grot

Parochial Technics

Lucifer Over Lancashire, made by BBC Community Programme Unit's *Open Door*, was part of a scheme which began in 1973, predating *Rising Damp* by a handful of months, and which allowed local people to posit and produce, with the help of a BBC community council — in the role of a kind of technical advisory synod — a documentary programme which responded to a pertinent local issue. Produced in 1987, by then re-named the *Open Space* unit, it still just about seems possible, trowelling through *Radio Times* sediment:

> *RADIO TIMES LISTING, MARCH 1987: More than 300 years after the Lancashire Witch Trials, The Rev Kevin Logan of Accrington rings alarm bells at the increase of interest in witchcraft in his area.*
>
> *Against the background of a Post-industrial wasteland a battle is being waged for the souls of the young.*
>
> *Local witches and satanists, however, fear that the campaign could become a latter-day witch-hunt. They claim that their religions are older than Christianity.*

Deep pagan yet post-industrial attributes propagate best in Reggie's suburbs (and its pubs): the extra-parochial zone, where you can practice rituals without undue persecution, set against the backdrop of patterned green and brown damp wallpaper. Grand Master Sylvanus of Lancashire Coven, and key occult spokesman in *Lucifer Over Lancashire* explains, whilst being interviewed at his suburban home: "a mob can't surround a semi-detached".

Battle Against the Satanists: where do they get these matching home furnishings?

Lucifer Over Lancashire's singularity is its occult thematic in conjunction with a localised production base and theme, after over thirty years of regional focus. Back in the prehistory of 1955, the new "Independent Television" (ITV) network was made up of numerous companies providing a regional television service. By the mid to late 1980s, with the neoliberal expansion, the medium that once represented visionary public broadcasting was subject to this onset of "occupying powers", as Denis Potter called them, in response to regional and global deregulation. The scope of this regional variation is described in a segment of Alan Partridge's latest TV series, *This Time* (2021), which sees him reporting on life in a young offender's institute. He reads the inmates backdated issues of the *TV Times* from the 1970s:

ALAN: You see, up until twenty years ago, ITV was split up into fifteen different franchises, so if you were in Leeds you'd be watching Yorkshire TV, in Newcastle that would be Tyne Tees. Where I'm from, it was Anglia.[1]
YOUNG INMATE: What the fuck are you on about?[2]

The deregulated and expanded availability of current real time channels' media hegemony equates to a contracted philosophy. As a sketch from *A Bit of Fry & Laurie* suggests, on the subject of broadcasting deregulation to encourage "*consumer choice*", Fry (as a waiter) pours a mountain of plastic spoons on a government minister's plate in response to his request for one set of silver cutlery (Series 2, Episode 5, 1990). To say nothing of the communal spatio-temporality of a television broadcast event prior to globalised TV patterns. Particular redolent in *Rising Damp* is the fact that the broadcast sitcom was an appointment kept by millions. TV was this time-specific event, with lodger's like Rigsby's crowded together round the box. While the standards of broadcasting now aim ever lower for market share, terrestrial TV as fantasy analogue dissipates in favour of personalised entertainment environments indurate to material strangeness, but bent to algorithmic private fantasies.

ALAN PARTRIDGE: My greatest broadcast achievement is my consistent resistance to dumbing down. I think if anything, I've tried to dumb up. (2021).

The duality of regional television posited against marketisation

1   A reminder of the Anglia mystery play.
2   Regional broadcasting in England was completely abolished in 2006.

and telecommunications' resultant collapsing of space-time is paratextually embodied in the Alan Partridge series itself, ironically emulating the latter half of a burnt-out TV presenter's career through the diversification of media platforms "in an increasingly fragmented marketplace", as Alan puts it himself, in a memo he accidentally reads live on the radio station North Norfolk Digital during his *Mid Morning Matters* show.

The "fragmented marketplace" of Accrington, returning to *Lucifer Over Lancashire,* is an oblique substratum, avowing a weird self-aware Holy Englishness seeping through in the replacement of a popular socialistic force. Crucially, the parochial vicar is the guide to the reginal episode, bringing Evangelism to the grubby porch step of extra-parochial "satanism" he fears is overrunning and poisoning the youths of the locale, whilst audio punctuation comes self-reflexively from the eponymous Fall track, itself lyrically a product of a Northern local newspaper story. The tune blurts in alongside repeated tableaus of kicked in TVs and wind-blown newspaper scraps amongst the garbage and carrier bags, bearing headlines: BATTLE AGAINST THE SATANISTS.

It is news as a popular form that unfolds from a harnessing of oral tradition, fiction, local myth and gore. From this, the street crier's ballad develops into what Lennard Davis has called the "news-novel matrix" where "newes" applies perfidiously well to both recent events, canards and supernatural occurrence. With Martin Luther's *Flugschriften*, the popular printed surface flies and unfurls through mediated time, finding its twentieth-century high-point in tabloids. Bringing together embodied experience with myth and delusion, if you follow Burroughs' assertion that the word and image, as channelled through newspapers, are powerful instruments of control.

Antiquarian herme(neu)tics channelled by Burroughs' cut-up was more frequently enacted, appositely, on newspaper text: "cut right through the pages of newsprint — cut up the headlines and a future, or the truth, truth, leaks out", he says. The repeated cut to shots of headlines in *Reginald Perrin* chart the *Rise* of his new business success: "Grot". This "rubbish chain" of shops, Reggie's "last defiant gesture to the world", developed towards the end of Series 2, is the lauding of all that is "utterly useless": a ludic tactic of commercial and geological undermining of both his professional misery, and spiritual languor. The dream of perverting consumer compulsion at its own game sees him open a shop selling his son-in-law's "absolutely revolting" turnip wine, square hoops, bad paintings of the Algarve, weightless weights, unstrung tennis rackets, inter alia, all ostensibly as unsellable Grot.

The Grot headlines heralding his idea's success appear written on branded metal lattice hoarding holders, as they also do in *Lucifer Over Lancashire*: weird place-markers, littering pavements outside corner shops.

"GROT DIVIDENT UP BY 20%" ... "RECORD PROFITS FOR RUBBISH CHAIN"

These headlines run the pages of *The Sunday Times* and *The Daily Express*, but their imbrication in fiction is nonetheless equivalent to the arcana of the local newspapers' fertile ground for a fragmented breakdown of reality systems at the level of truth and fiction, such that the fabulated and torn newspaper headlines tumbling across the barren landscape in *Lucifer* were always rogation ceremony markers of the extra-parochial's causational zones, with the local paper being an exemplary parochial technic for this dissemination.

Détourning christianity with its pagan-inflected headline

place-markers, the ghoulish *Lucifer* headlines are scraps of magical writing frittering around Accrington and outside Reggie's corner shops: the conjuring of a dissipative, damp spell to question common knowledge and revive a decaying present.

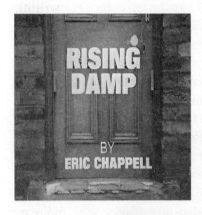

Bricking it with magical spells — n/ooze of routine distributed across rubbish surfaces.

Accrington's local newspapers swirling with magical stories recharge reality with the humorous buzz of possibility, underlined by the transformative power of the Lancashire landscape itself. Like the marsh, it's a bleak and melancholy transhistorical zone to which repeated patterns of evil and aberrant behaviours are drawn.[3] The self-fulfilling headlines operative as prophesies languish as transitory graffiti in gutters outside Woolworths: motile inscription of the more ancient effects of place. A moving scrap heap, a moving writing of the earth, attaching and detaching from the landscape. Where damp is the patina of time, of history as the haunted materialisation of existential compromise, text here in the fragmented headlines is a de(sur)facement of the parochial, its fragments flitting across landscapes. Haunting the stain of (the) place (of Runwell), Revd Rainaldus from Running Well prefigures the enfolding of site as technology, the *Ur*-form, the newspaper's oozing news of routine (or indeed its n/ooze) bubbling on the surface without which we'd "ooze all over the floor", as Rigsby suggests.[4] The collision of "newes" as a version of the parochial leaflet after the fiery clamour of has died out, that cuts an archaeological hole through the forgotten windswept precincts of Accrington.

YOUTH OF ACCRINGTON: The Industrial Revolution has come and gone, and people are trying to fill that vacuum with something else. They are looking for transcendental cures.

---

3   "More than 300 years after the Lancashire witch trials, the Rev. Kevin Logan of Accrington rings alarm bells at the increase of interest in witchcraft in his area".

4   Ramun, a Lancashire High Priest of the Northern Order of the Prince, knits ancient text to derelict communities via technology: "Our scriptures, the *Raz Cathab Mashall* [sic] are very ancient documents, and we've had to put them on computer to make sure they survive the rigours of time".

Like the youth of Accrington, a ludic yet mystical pharmakon is sought in the miasma of excoriating commerce, and its flattening effects, for which Reggie "forever revolting" Perrin dreamt up Grot. The youth, flashing fruit machine lights glimmering in the background as he sits in the boozer, explains that "somewhere in the human mind in the key to our existence". The *Pandaemonium* of the senses that re-write the landscape had reached a mid-century terminus: *Reggie Over Surbiton* finds in the newspaper an unwitting McGuffin too, folded under the arm each morning, when he gives a fake headline to Mrs Perrin (played by Pauline Yates) in the light of whatever comment she makes as he leaves the house: "I can see the headlines now: *WIFE SAVES DORMITORY TOWN FROM ZIP HORROR.*"

His repeated walk through the Romantic cul-de-sac is a space where Reggie's hallucinated fictions are acted out, and he flashes the old woman. *What does any of it matter?* he asks (his body bent like a question mark). Recalling ancient Egyptian place-based mythemes that relate the spatial and the local as a sacred universal, Reggie repeatedly walks through the ritual walkway of Poets Estate, traversing *Coleridge Close, Tennyson Avenue, Wordsworth Drive*. The newspaper crossword is terraced to the commute: the repetitive timestamp of train delays, scripted by the inner voice. A nondescript ditch in Essex, some trouser flies in Norbiton, vouchsafes Gnostic fabulation, germinated in parochial methods of pilgrimage.

This is uniquely linked to the fleeting headlines too, the occulted scraps in the vicinity of rubbish, or the waste paper bins. The local newspaper as the psychometric object, legend to nodal outbursts of text and outrage that peel off the past and crawl into the furrows, are adroit visual clue to Reggie's

Bin herme(neu)tics in Lucifer over Lancashire.

metaphysical base matter. Newspapers are, according to John Dryden: *martyrs to pies and relics of the bum* — street garbage and public trash, where our lives and imprints make fleeting surface support: mini battles fought over a torn paper, connecting many histories, impressions, places. "*What About Us?*" as Mark E. Smith asks, in the lyrics that concur with this proximity in heightened fragments of text: "*But then one night by the green grass, By a rubbish receptacle, I saw a newspaper, I was not very happy…*" (2004). The method equates to a radical contingency again. Like the magical headlines, Grot is, as Reggie's advert states for his new business, "*The Place for Rubbish*".

> *REGGIE: Every single thing in this shop is guaranteed absolutely useless.*

The genesis of Grot comes from a meeting between Reggie and his "cock up on the catering front" ex-army brother-in-law Jimmie. The episode "Jimmie's Offer", details a grimy and clandestine meeting of the two in Jimmy's "Bed Sitter" to meet his "secret agent" — a rifle in a box under his bed, with which he is going to muster a private army and begin a counter-revolution.

> *REGGIE: Who on earth are these for?*
> *JIMMY: Army equipped to fight for Britain when the balloon goes up.*

This itself was a non-fiction lifted from the matrix of newes by writer David Nobbs. On ITV in 1974 and 1977, right-winger Jimmy Green used his position as presenter of TV talent show *Opportunity* (remove yourself from your grimy desperation) *Knocks* to soapbox for a "renewed" Britain. Paramilitary groups were said to be organising in the British countryside against Harold Wilson's perceived socialism — or worse, Soviet agency — in a weird and paranoid stew espoused by Green, who turns to the camera, rupturing the "television situation" of the light entertainment show, and in flagrant breach of the 1955 Broadcasting Act (which stipulated that political issues should be dealt with on television with due impartiality) and, with the swell of the orchestra behind him, sombrely tells the audience in the studio and at home: "Let us work with all our might to see that 1975, with the gathering storm of despair ahead, will not be the end of our country. Lest we perish, friends, let us all together say in 1975, both to the nation, to each other and to ourselves: for God's sake, Britain, wake up!"

Green's speech, *Stand Up and Be Counted*, proselytises as Revd Kevin Logan, of St John's Church Great Harwood Parish's "Christian battle waged in North East Lancashire fought on many fronts."

The noxious atmosphere occasions a lurid contrast with *Rising Damp*, too. Where Rigsby's misanthropic posturing were occasionally loveable, Jimmy's war is a weirder proposition. A predictable response to the denuding of life's meaning. The excess of Jimmy's desperate manifesto has the tedium of an endless saint's litany, as much as being a strange antidote to Reggie's earlier rant at the executives at the work speech — "are we getting our just desserts?"

> *REGGIE: What Army? What balloon? Up what? Fight against whom? Come on Jimmy, who are you going to fight against when this balloon goes up?*
> *JIMMY: Force of anarchy. Wreckers of law and order.*
> *REGGIE: Oh, I see.*
> *JIMMY: Communists, Maoists, Trotskyists, neo-Trotskyists, crypto-Trotskyists, union leaders, Communist union leaders, atheists, agnostics, long-haired weirdos, short-haired weirdos, vandals, hooligans, football supporters, namby-pamby probation officers, rapists, papists, papist rapists, foreign surgeons, headshrinkers — who ought to be locked up — Wedgwood Benn, keg bitter, punk rock, glue-sniffers, 'Play For Today', squatters, Clive Jenkins, Roy Jenkins, Up Jenkins, up everybody's, Chinese restaurants — why do you think Windsor Castle is ringed with Chinese restaurants?*
> *REGGIE: I see, is that all? You realise the sort of people you're going to attract, don't you Jimmy? Thugs, bully-boys, psychopaths, sacked policemen, security guards, sacked security guards, racialists, Paki-bashers, queer-bashers, Chink-bashers, anybody- bashers, bashers-bashers, Rear Admirals, queer Admirals, Vice Admirals, fascists, neo-fascists, crypto-fascists, loyalists, neo-loyalists, crypto-loyalists.*
> *JIMMY: Do you think so? I thought recruitment might be difficult. Well Reggie, are you with us?*
> *REGGIE: I certainly am not; I have never heard such absolute rubbish. It is all rubbish. It is absolute and utter rubbish. Not only that, Jimmie, it is neo-rubbish and crypto-rubbish. Rubbish… Rubbish… RUBBISH!*

Shouting "rubbish" is when the penny drops for Reggie. He is going to subvert homogenous culture by selling rubbish back to it: Grot.

REGGIE: Well, we're sold so much rubbish these days under false pretences, I decided to be honest about it.

Reggie is seen painting the words "Grot" on his first shop window — and thereafter a montage of high street stock images *détourned* with the Grot logo demonstrate the rapid spread of his empire. This strange headline is a fortune-telling parish noticeboard, with words that herald in the pink and green effervescent bloom of dripping damp, the calamity it might foretell.

Noise 6

Chuckle Brothers in Southend Part 2 (not Adam Bohman version) detail: leaving Cliffs Pavilion in their camper van and heading towards Hamlet Court Road, followed with hand held CCTV... sufficient unto the day is the evil thereof... Meet you in the Mile and a Third in that road, last known sighting... straight on until closing time...

Reprographic Disappointments

The dichotomy of Grot's success and Reggie's failure is the doyen of the gurgling Code. Grot may have been dreamt up as inutile and unproductive expenditure, but its legend is written across huge representative structures of psychic commerce: the selling mechanism of the huge advert.

Grot's advertisement is a huge white billboard, its legend in twentieth-century damp given away in the deliquescent slime heralded in large, pink, snot-dripping letters across the huge advert poster. Earlier examples of advertising in *Reggie Perrie* include the huge billboard outside Sunshine Desserts: *Try Sunshine flans — they're FLANtastic*. The routine drudgery of this copy is reflected in the litany of pointless marketing activities performed at his work, as the nadir of technology's magical thinking and divinatory possibilities:

> *REGGIE: If we're finished ice cream testing, Tony here will collect your cards and we'll have the verdict from the computer before you can say prune and pumpkin Neapolitan.*

Good commuter line.

Advertising jargon is designed to penetrate the subconscious mind, to cause a person to do something they might not do otherwise. It is unsurprising that the proliferation of images, unto the present, has been both led by and directed the language of advertisement: multiplying like parasitic worms, such grot pops up across the landscape, seeking to dominate the environment. Contained in the wooden frame, but arguably unleashed virtually intravenously through contemporary forms of algorithmic marketing. Akin to the Grot mythos of rubbish as sacred base matter, advertising itself is excessive uncontainable, matter, a language that takes over reality; it posits itself as natural, something real — it is dislodged desire as pieces of fragmented old paper, writhing in the wind.

"Paul and Barry become Advertisers and are asked to plaster a billboard".

REGGIE: Would you be kind enough to give us your market report, Miss Pigeon?
ESTHER: Yes. 71% of housewives in East Lancashire and 81% in Hertfordshire expressed an interest in the concept of exotic ice-creams. Only 8% in Hertfordshire and 14% in Lancashire

expressed positive hostility, whilst 5% expressed latent hostility. In Hertfordshire, 96% of the 50% who formed 20% of consumer spending were in favour. 0.6% told us where we could put our exotic ice creams.

Strange hoardings are generative billboard disappointments, such as that which appears in an episode of *The Chuckle Brothers*: true shamans of the parochial. Text in their 1990 episode "Poster Pranks" is fragmented, ruptured on the support surface. In their misadventures with installation, they bridge the decrepitude of life with a darker residue: Grot, or indeed, the Carnival Grotesque: the comic metaphysics of horror and mundanity. The horror of this consciousness is what even the Chuckle Brothers can run with: life is meaningless, and they know it, but a glimpse from the "Muddy Friend" is reward enough for these labours.

REGGIE: It is all rubbish. It is absolute and utter rubbish. Not only that, Jimmie, it is neo-rubbish and crypto-rubbish. Rubbish... Rubbish... RUBBISH!

The advert sheets on a large billboard are splayed in large wooden frames like the alchemist's linen sheets propped up on small stakes, as seen in *Mutus Liber* (Mute Book), published in La Rochelle, in 1677: stretch surface supports for collecting the dew, to use in the Great Work. These uneven rolls of fabric are cut from the same methodological cloth as Fr. Rolfe's stained arras, which also soak up the power of damp's historicity. Apophatic headlines on newspapers and advert hoardings are traces of revelation.

In his new office at Perrin Products (Grot Ltd.), Reggie continues the branding. The huge, raised company logo a terrible bas-relief: a Cthulhu-like lump of hallucinatory lore, to accompany the sacrificial altar of the photocopier megalith. What if the marsh is photocopied to scale, for his billboard campaign? If photocopied, ancient presences will seep through old copy toner. The vast expanse of mythographic landscape consciousness as broken and anti-representational Grot, written large across Essex as the ultimate technological surface, for all its surrealist flashy consumerism. A bin voyage across the real enlarged hyperbolic terrain that a shaman like Reginal Perrin manifests.

It has a moribund appearance, the photocopier in my old newspaper job *The Leigh Times* office, and in Reggie's office: like an office menhir, a sacred site to decrypt a surface, a mid-twentieth-century meets prehistoric burial light box, premised on its analogue grainy materiality. These ancient structures, such as the one at New Grange in Ireland, and delineated as such by Michael O'Kelly in 1963, had an entrance arranged such that a thin beam of sunlight would pass therein during the Solstice, into the crypt: a scanning tablet surface on the Winter Solstice. Like a large photocopier, the beam catches the dust motes in the air of the tomb: a ritual standing stone in a burial complex of the office, where the bulb of the scanner light is the illuminating beam of sunlight, activating something metastable within the site.

The photocopier-crypt animates the seemingly-dead, like a sitcom laughter track. Such laughter tracks through the marsh, and the mud likewise, putting a cuneiform tablet on the scanning bed of the bulky office menhir, the *Ur*-stumbling block as the originary technical object to activate the landscape, carries this germ of comedy. If the scanner animates the undead laughter, it plays the sitcom *Carry On Cuneiform*. The letters themselves across the clay ground are a writing of light and dark itself: it's only the shadows, when slanted against the light, which reveal the incisions — a kind of shadow ink. A script now adumbrated by the bulbs, circuits, panels of a flickered scanning. The cuneiform becomes a productive technological node, a mysterious site of the time's dissimulation, at work as de(sur)facement of the photocopied page.

Cuneiform photocopy: Waddell happen next?

In Bataillean fashion, Grot is commensurate to old office paraphernalia, wheezing photocopier, shoddy attitudes, ludic clowning, a lauding of the *inutile* — a reprographic disappointment which also plays on the loathed and muddy *waste* land of the marsh. A reminder that unworking has a granular purchase: one that goes beyond a puerile joke of cuneiform. The spluttering creaking machine, the necessary jam in the smooth rhythm of mechanised method of pre-digital reproducibility, the re-inscription of the surface choked through spluttering toner, that doesn't come out properly, charting a syncopated rhythm, a malfunctioning, a subverting of heterogeneity, like Bataille's "excess... that tries to jam or block the machine". A humour close to terror, the hideous drab hilarity of an office, and importantly, the Bataillean "unproductive expenditure" of making artwork on the photocopier, when you're meant to be working: a tactic reminiscent of Reggie himself.

C.J.: I didn't get where I am without knowing a completely useless machine when I see one.

Its potentials, despite being invented through a patent attorney, changed the site and production of autonomous knowledge. This "green-eyed deus ex machina", as Donald Morrison, in his essay "What hath XEROX Wrought?', from 1976 — the year *Reginald Perrin* aired — says, has compromised authorship to the extent that it's "punched holes in copyright law": parochial technics create a thousand-year stare, a bullet in the right place, to tunnel back to the marsh. In Alan Partridge's *Knowing Me, Knowing You* (1994), a machine is wheeled on-set to dumbfound and humiliate a hubristic actor and erstwhile photocopy repairman during his chat show interview: of course, the trouble is that it's "jammed".

To Me, To You.

ALAN: Will you rise to Alan's challenge and mend the photocopier?
GARY: Of course I can mend, it. What model is it?
ALAN: Z60.
GARY: Mono or Multi-feed?
ALAN: Mono-feed.
GARY: Easy.
ALAN: Prove it!
GARY: It hasn't been re-set after a paper jam. Basic.

The clue is in Grot's perspicacious tagline: "<u>The</u> Place for Rubbish". Equating, again, gnosis to location, navigable in the most spiritual of technology: from the commute with its adverts and newspaper, to the office and its photocopier and the backwards home on the commute with its backwards adverts, whipping by, back always to the marsh.

What grotty adverts would Reggie have seen on his train line, freewheeling him into industrial folklore? Perhaps this one from 1976: "I've changed to No.6 Extra Players — the low-tar cigarette you can stay with". The philosophy of urban modernism has shaped the mundane locales with these hoardings, and painted sides of buildings — the former just visible still as a commercial ghost, a painted de(sur)facement on Victorian structures. Grot's success is in part down to the Grot of adverts, and the adverts of Grot. Starting in part to risibly mirror the commercial imperatives of his old firm Sunshine Desserts, despite being a community undevoured by market mechanics, Grot ends up a £750,000 success, through the advertising campaigns of the idiotic son-in-law, Tom, and its ensuing TV ad campaign that have "become a national cult", as Reggie's wife describes them. The Grot logo appears on the glass TV screen like a vast televised cuneiform tablet, before subliminal black-and-white handwritten flashes of "Grot Sales Now" flicker through the awfully acted shop scene of the advert: another attempt by the advertising industry to inveigle into the psyche. Reggie had employed Tom, as much as Doc Morrissey, Jimmy and an Irishman called Seamus, because he felt assured of their "grotty" incompetence. Figured to help him "destroy the Monster" or "empire" that he has created. Reggie's behaviours whilst being CEO of Grot are in turn harlequinesque, taciturn, unthought-out.

REGGIE: To tell you the truth, I started the whole thing off as a joke. I'd spent a quarter of a century in puddings and I was feeling a trifle stifled. So, I decided to try something else — I started Grot. But now I'm much more interested in my bankruptcy.

Seaside de(sur)facement.

Backfiring on him, Reggie is "fed up with success of Grot", as the credit legend reads in Series 2, Episode 7, "Extreme Solution". Guidance that an inversion of shallow merchandised reality cannot replace the office of the soul. The failsafe squalor of *Code: Damp* is belied, always, by the real power of both capitalism, and base matter, which is Grot by any other word; the legend of subsumption to all cultural forms of aberration fall. In trying to sell something unsellable, Reggie capitulates to capitalism's code. Recall that Reggie's own anti-globalised tirade at the Bilbury Hall fruit association speech was itself derided as such.

> DR HUMP: *(mutters to Mr Watkins): This is rubbish. (Reggie overhears)*
> REGGIE: *More rubbish, that's a very good point, thank you, Hump.*

Reggie screeching into chaos again, creating a *sit-storm*. Strange crop circles are rising up under the suburbs. Damp's Code crawling up Tudorbethan guttering, French windows cracking, green patterns on the infested curtains reforming into cuneiform letters...

Noise 7
I think we've reached the party layer… Parish Use Only…

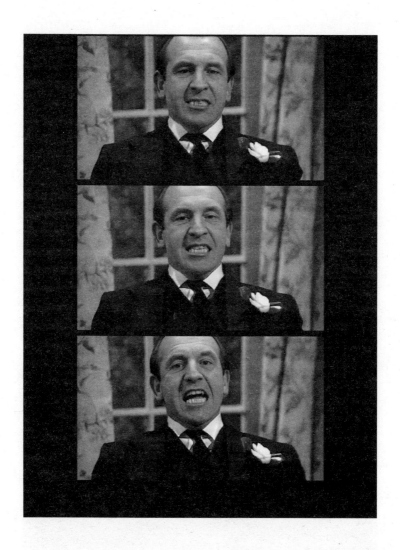

201

Noise 8
Things are hotting up in the car park. Time: Tomorrow... Like being a substitute in a football match...

The Scream

Indurate to the commercial imperative, Grot's advertisements seek something greater than financial remuneration or the passive consumption of the present. Image and text conspire to betray a fault line in *Code: Damp*'s ancient metaphysical hunger: Reginald Perrin's scream. This moment, which occurs at the END of Episode 1 of Series 1, equates to a ludic exorcism of the 1970s. A weapon to make a hole in the infested fabric of the everyday.

Thriller (1974) ITV.

As a freeze-frame, it is the very finest in inarticulate pressure-valve release. Is this a nihilistic breakdown, a detached alienation, a symbolic negativity? He breathes marsh miasma into the airlessness of the self(obsessed)-help literature: a hole pierced in that which is so often the lectionary of the contemporary individual. As mass-culture magician, he is a counter to the proliferation of self-appointed lifestyle gurus and online wellness culture, fusing hippy spirituality and late consumerism. This spread of the self-appointed is a gravedigger mimicry of consumer-counterculture liberation, perpetuating online augur's cant to "Egyptianise", in Nietzsche's terms, the *élan vital*.

RIGSBY: You don't like walking through the graveyard at night.

This is the sorry terminus of marshy current abroad during the fecund 1960s, a facet outlined by Perrin's awful "commune" that he starts in Series 3. Coming at a time when arguably Rigsby's tenants' post-1968 counter-cultural affectation was slipping away into thin set of neoliberal lifestyle choices.[1] Reggie's scream, echoing through our latter-day screen bewitchment, is not the mid-century "Primal Scream", popularised in the 1970s by the epiphanous book by Arthur Janov. Published six years before the sitcom's broadcast, Reggie's is an alternative to the individualistic transformation promised by alternative psychiatry during this decade, but is in no doubt is a wry nod thereto, touching on the spectres of the time, whilst mobilising darker frameworks within the suburban carapace. In the mildew theatre of class consciousness, Reggie meets R.D. Laing at the curtain call of counter-culture, with Reggie at once a warning and a willing obliteration: dedication not medication, industrial antagonism as opposed to lifestyle affect.

Gargoyle

Reggie screams in ludic fury at the repetitive tedium of his life in the very first episode of the series. But the scream, insisting on a need to dramatise existence in general, is just as relevant at the end of the entire run, in 1979, as he comes "Full Circle". The scream, through which a temporally antagonistic multiplicity of inhuman pulses speak, is a magical technic through which the self-same is divested, but through which a repetition is also evident. With the sitcom line up of grotesques — albeit cardboard cut-out characters with their catchphrases: C.J. and the office workers — lies the darker fount of an existential horror of life, from which the scream is corroboration and diversion, as much as it is a "[non] lyrical

---

1 "Bollocks to Yoga", writes Austin Osman Spare in his late 1940s occult manuscript *Logomachy of Zos*.

protest", operative as a kind of Situationist *dérive* through the human limit.

The open mouth is often interpreted as a dilation of space-time, termed the "syncope", from *synkoptein*, "to cut up", a common tool in the mystics' arsenal, with the effect of a "miraculous suspension" of self. Cautioning against both shallow versions of the self and the personalised entertainment environments of a mantra-numbed present. Marsh stasis is a momentary cut-up, a scream from the landscape, revealing a generosity of expression at odds with Acéphale's secrecy — the Greek word *myein*, for closed mouth or eyes at the heart of mystery cults, is that which has not been, or cannot be, explained. Suspension of the self is on the other hand an abnegation of sorts, a self-sacrifice as a re-writing of the self, a share in the ongoing deracination of cuneiform: one of "those who inscribe new values on new tablets", says Nietzsche.

Not only a horror trope or mystical dilation, the mouth is a commuter train tunnel, or a deep *well* through which an embodied stream of psycho-topographical Mud Flat Time flows. Georges Bataille's definition of "sewer" in the 1947 *Encyclopaedia Da Costa* suggests it being a source of "sacrifices and magic [...] we no longer know". *Carry On At*

BBC M.R. James gargoyle, Anno Damp 1974.

Your Convenience rather suggests Reggie is a parish gargoyle. From the old French *gargouille*, "throat", the stone and marble creations were so-called because of the water passing through the throat and mouth as an elaborate ecclesiastical plumbing.

Felix Barker reviewed Leonard Rossiter in an edition of *Evening News* in 1969, asking *"has there been such a grotesquery since the hunchbacked Loughton swung from the gargoyles of Notre Dame?"*.

The gargoyle is a remnant of English "Arcady" clinging to cathedrals, a necessary Rabelaisian mash-up of pulp and more readily indexed Christian authority and Jocund Pagan in the pub ephemera of the Green Man. As a ghoul presiding over the rogation ceremony, or a neat teatime idol serving folk horror's mildewed fancies, Reggie is this pulp gargoyle, turning time into space via TV plumbing, stretching back to the Archē. The floral wallpaper and Brit stereotypes, proof of modernity's channelling of spirit into the straightjacket of street planning, fast food and force-fed culture, hide the reality of Mesopotamian hop-counting, a dredging-back to a post-Lutheran mysticism, the recording of the scream played from damp remnant on marsh reeds.

Talking of a role Leonard Rossiter plays in 1972 for HTV, Philip Purser, in *The Sunday Telegraph*, says: "Rossiter's shifty, insecure, peg-toothed grin was, like the locale, absolutely specific and therefore universal." Like the extra-parochial as a model for modernity's mysticism, his scream interrupts predictive processes of subjectivation in the present by *localising* this ghastly drain, whilst invoking the hallucination of epochal conditions: providing access on a slipstream of time travel out of historicity on its own material terms, for re-entry into a renewed multidirectional and elemental reality — both in the diegesis of the sitcom and shimmering logic outside of it.

Damp's Code is both Reggie's release and return, Fall and Rise. Following on from the pivotal scream that heads the whole series, the final episode, "Full Circle", results in his return to an almost identical work place, with the same boss. The names of the street names are now less English Romanticism, more existential realisation: a definite turn-up for the books. He walks past *Leibnitz Drive*, *Bertrand Russell Rise*, *Schopenhauer Grove*.

If Rigsby in *Rising Damp* was the odea of damp's ingress into culture, the de(sur)faced support for it to work its necessary patina, Reggie in *Fall and Rise* is the symbol of the consumer beset with commercial imperatives, but one who can blast out of regulated torpor by facing head on the duality of capitalism. Reggie's scream is its preternatural billboard image of this "unacceptable face": both augur of later hyper-industrialisation and ancient nuisance. Rigsby's mystical art of living, and now Reggie's faked death and scream, is dedication to magical tactics.

Same Time, Same Channel: *Saluté*!

Rossiter's re-enchantment of landscape works both backward and forwards; it's because the 1970s coalesce the elemental substratum of all of damp's iterations, from Mesopotamia, through the furnace, archaeological logic, and the Essex well. Representative of, and access to, the hinterland of the marsh, the sitcom elides the edge lands of landscape with the hinterlands of society and culture in popular pulp, and the personal hypnagogic relation of its mysticism. The two sitcoms do this because of both atmospheric and material conditions and humours of damp — now increasingly spurned and castigated — and because of their situation at a threshold moment, where pre-globalist cultural forms and modes of being could still be felt through broad sweeps of society, before their rapid crumbling under a techno-cultural assault on space-time: the very basis upon which damp is understood. A contemporary system measures the decomposition of audience's digital data to prophesy trends and streamed content without the tele-vision that an engrained patina reproduces. Saturation for the former, gutted of contingent force, fails to capitalise on the cuneiform decomposition at heart of Archē Damp's bricolage.

On his psychic commute to the marsh, that is also, still, neither truly pro- or anti-globalisation, Perrin doesn't decide to return, but is compelled or drawn into the deviant Code that Damp engrains: access to the hinterland. "Full Circle" in the last episode is the circular time of Howerd's *Up Pompeii!* which begins — and ends — with *The Prologue.* It's the circle of the Mystery Play Cycle: often a trinity of three dramas, played simultaneously, detailing the Creation, The Passion and Doomsday.

The scream collapses *this* book's trinity of site place and de(sur)facement: read as the 1970s, the sitcom and damp. A collapse as the motif of mystical autobiography for both Rigsby, Rossiter and Reggie. Such mystical autobiography is recursively founded on Modernity's simultaneous blurring and separation of reality and myth. The marsh's cut-up is one incantation of Modernity's dissipative reality system.

This is how grainy 1970s artefacts parse the weird portal of the internet, the inner narrative, fragmentary as it is, foregrounds an innately cuneiform consciousness. In this exposure of an abject vulnerability in the face of its atomisation, when all pretence at being able to defend oneself has been abandoned, Reggie's scream knuckles down on duration and strength of character. In ersatz nowhere, Reggie mimes perennial motion inward to the muddy companion, and outward to the world of structures and schemes designed to bend the soul to its designs: a "perennial" farcing of mystical theology, and a knowingly absurd gesture in this respect. Its *Code: Damp*'s central unifying image for a new myth based on the marsh sitcom.

My aim is that *Code: Damp* might be found in decades to come, in an old pub in Essex somewhere, a forgotten pamphlet on a shelf, a Lutheran *Flugschriften* considered the soiled and strange ramblings of a post-industrial estuary cult. Scampi Fries will huddle in their plastic packet like oedemic cuneiform sherds. Holsten will be magically back on tap in the pub as beer analogue to the fate of sitcom, to the changing whirlpool of how the world is and was. The pub will be the sacred site for this event, the mystical alignment that allows the marsh to be a zone of causational happenings again, where writing flows through damp's power.[2]

MARK E. SMITH: This is where true penmanship stamina comes into its own as by now, guilt, drunkenness, the people in the pub and the fact you're one of them should combine to enable you to write out of sheer vexation. (The Mark E. Smith Guide to Writing Guide).

The Code never stops. Never ends. The subhuman voices will carry on, will inveigle the duration of your day, will worm

---

2   A great deal of my writing happened in pubs, incl. of my PhD: thanks, to Westcliff's *Mile and a Third*, cf. *The London Drinker* Vol.45 No.3, June/ July 2023: 21–23.

through the billboards, the genesis of the industrialised world of factory, office, and pub. Old cuneiform letters haemorrhage into the page you're now reading, sensing the world's flesh ready to reach out to the mephitic Babylonian winds on a TV side of your choice, once the brittle glamour of the present starts to peel away. In the concluding words of Frankie Howerd's episode-ending *Prologue*[3]: *Same Time, Same Channel: Saluté!*

---

3 I am now wondering if *Whoops Baghdad*, Howerd's ill-fated follow up to *Up Pompeii!* (slated to be originally called *Up Iraq*) should have been considered.

The Prologue

Leonard Rossiter may well have even once visited a marsh landscape, a scene I can only see through cathode-ray tube vision, a precondition of the technology's effect in the psyche. In this distant land, you forge a meaningful imprint on  the mud, to make you feel the beat and lag of existence in the ruins of disenchanted rubble. This is how the heavy sodden records of industrial Light Entertainment provides joyous transit through its own necessary strip-lit corridors. Thought ceases to be separated from delirium in the ultimate aim of *Code: Damp*. The bleeding of life into work:

Rossiter is caught on train station CCTV at Southend station, heading for the marshes: the muddy landscape at the heart of this esoteric-materialist world. In a theatricalisation of the parish, he strides along the marsh embankment, carrier bag in hand. Scrabbling in its purple printed plastic, he's an anachronistic relic drunk on the marsh's mousy *krausen*. He cracks the can, hands gnawed in the marsh fog, looks to the camera. Akkadian subtitles run along the bottom of the screen: "Keep taking the Pils."

Acknowledgements

I would like to thank my editor, Tariq Goddard, for understanding the weird necessity of this project. For their help realising it, I thank James Hunt, Josh Turner and Christopher DeVeau at Repeater Books. Thank you to James Sirrell for reading and discussing umpteen drafts with candour and vim, and to Lurach John Bredin for inhabiting the mythos through many essential conversations. For his ongoing encouragement I thank my erstwhile PhD supervisor, Michael Newman, and for (pel)lucid kelp pit kinship, m'colleague Jon K. Shaw. Thank you to my mother, Susan Sleigh-Johnson, for both her unquenchable joie-de-cava and her cheering company on numerous pilgrimages to locations herein. Thank you also to my father, David Kettle, for a comprehensive induction into the VHS gnosis of TV comedy.

REPEATER BOOKS

is dedicated to the creation of a new reality. The landscape of twenty-first-century arts and letters is faded and inert, riven by fashionable cynicism, egotistical self-reference and a nostalgia for the recent past. Repeater intends to add its voice to those movements that wish to enter history and assert control over its currents, gathering together scattered and isolated voices with those who have already called for an escape from Capitalist Realism. Our desire is to publish in every sphere and genre, combining vigorous dissent and a pragmatic willingness to succeed where messianic abstraction and quiescent co-option have stalled: abstention is not an option: we are alive and we don't agree.